TROY DIXON

John's Letters

Sermon Summary Series

First published by Troy Dixon 2025

First edition

This book was professionally typeset on Reedsy.
Find out more at reedsy.com

Contents

Preface

The *Sermon Summary Series* is just what the title suggests: not full manuscripts, but more than bare outlines. My preaching usually grows out of what I call a "fat outline." That means I build the sermon around a structured framework, filling in carefully crafted sentences where precision matters, while leaving other sections as short reminders of thoughts I've shared often enough to flow naturally.

What you'll find here are outlines that have been expanded to the point where they can be read and followed with clarity. They stand as a record of my preaching ministry and, I pray, as a source of encouragement and edification to all who read them.

Every sermon in this collection is the fruit of careful study, prayer, and preparation. While plagiarism is abhorrent to me, I freely acknowledge the influence of countless writers, preachers, and professors whose words have shaped my own. Throughout these pages, I hope you hear the echoes of faithful theologians, historians, and pastors who have left their mark on my understanding of God's Word. For their labors, I am deeply and permanently grateful.

1

1 John 1:1-4

A highlight of my week is opening these boxes and reading the Gospel Conversation reports. Hearing how other believers share their faith and encourage others with prayer and the gospel is a joy. Our numbers have increased as we have been faithful in sharing, but that is not the primary motivation for sharing.

- Engaging in Gospel Conversations displays love and obedience for the Lord Jesus.
- Engaging in Gospel Conversations allows the Holy Spirit to develop our faith and maturity.
- Engaging in Gospel Conversations helps us learn the needs of people.
- Engaging in Gospel Conversations reminds us of the glory of the gospel.

We begin a new series through 1st John. According to history, he wrote his gospel, but false teachers were distorting its message, prompting him to write his first letter. He addresses the true nature of the Messiah. He addresses the true nature of our salvation. Much like the gospel of John, this is a simple but profound book. It is easy to understand, but the message resonates with us long after we have laid our Bibles down.

GOSPEL CONVERSATIONS
1 John 1:1-4

To understand the message of John's words today, we need to consider how he wrote them. Let's evaluate the structure of these four verses.

One of the keys to understanding a "didactic" passage—a teaching letter—is to locate the verbs. The writer is calling for or forbidding action. The "who" and the "what" are undoubtedly important, but the action is the key.

"We proclaim." It is present tense and active. It means this is what we are doing—and will continue to do. It is plural, meaning this is what all believers are to be doing.

He first describes the content of the proclamation: *"That which was from the beginning"* echoes Genesis 1:1 and John 1:1. It reminds us that Jesus is the eternal God who always has been. He also says he has heard, seen, and touched the Lord. It is a reminder that Jesus is the incarnate God he had met and known.

John was confronting a false theology that said salvation is through a "secret knowledge" that God bestows upon a small few. The Gnostics believed all matter was inherently evil, but John says this righteous God revealed himself in the flesh.

John isn't writing from theory. John proclaims what he knows about Jesus so that others may know Him, too. He isn't speaking of abstract theology. He's writing as someone who saw Jesus, heard His voice, and touched Him with his hands. And now, John wants us to know why he proclaims this truth—why we should, too.

Let's consider three elements of the message we proclaim to the world...

WE PROCLAIM THE LIFE OF JESUS (1:1-2)

John begins by describing the Word of life—the eternal Son of God—who was "from the beginning." He heard Him speak. He saw Him with his eyes. He touched Him with his hands. This is no imaginary Savior; this is the real, risen Jesus Christ. That's important because it means Jesus isn't a myth or a symbol. He lived in real time and space.

- Jesus experienced the *joys* of life- He likely loved the smell of fresh coffee, sunshine on His face, and watching babies learn to walk.
- Jesus experienced the *grief* of life—He grew hungry, walked everywhere, and likely had a sunburn. He was betrayed.
- Jesus experienced the *pain* of death—Religious leaders pushed Him through an unjust trial and crucified Him.

"HE GETS US" is an ad campaign during the Super Bowl. The television ads are part of a national campaign aimed at reintroducing Jesus to a modern, often skeptical or disconnected audience—particularly those who may feel disillusioned with organized religion but remain spiritually curious or searching. Their main message is that *Jesus understands our struggles, pain, challenges, and humanity. He gets us.* The ad has a tone that is compassionate, empathetic, and non-judgmental.

John is speaking about his testimony. I KNOW the truth of Jesus because I have lived the truth of Jesus.

Three points of application:

1. **Remember that your testimony is powerful.** You may not have seen Jesus physically like John, but you've encountered Him spiritually. Your story matters.
2. **Ground your faith in the truth of Christ.** The gospel isn't just emotional encouragement—it's rooted in real, historical events.

3. **Proclaim Christ from your own experience.** People don't need perfect arguments; they need honest testimonies. "This is who Jesus is and what He's done in me."

WE PROCLAIM THE NEED OF HUMANITY (1:3)

Invite people to church and listen to their responses. Approximately 50% are already affiliated with a church or have no interest in a church. The other 50% wonder if they will be welcomed. Do they have the right clothes? Will their tattoos be rejected? Are single moms or multiple divorced men welcome?

John speaks in this verse of *fellowship*. It is a word that goes deeper than mere friendship. It means "To share something in common." We are invited to share life, purpose, and joy with God and His people. God didn't design us to live disconnected from Him or others. God created us for relationships. That's why life feels so empty without purpose and why broken relationships hurt so deeply—it's because God made us for more."

Many people know something's off in their lives but can't quite name it. Scripture calls it sin—and it creates a barrier between us and God and between us and others. Something inside all of us knows things aren't right. That's not just circumstance—it's separation. Sin cuts us off from the relationship God created us to enjoy. But the good news is Jesus came to restore that fellowship—to reconnect us with the God who loves us."

- If our greatest need had been information, God would have sent us an educator.
- If our greatest need had been technology, God would have sent us a scientist.
- If our greatest need had been money, God would have sent us an economist.
- If our greatest need had been pleasure, God would have sent us an entertainer.
- But our greatest need was forgiveness, so God sent us a Savior.

Three points of application:

1. **Evangelism is not coercion—it's an invitation.** We're not selling something. We're saying, "Come and see what we've found."
2. **Don't just invite people to church—invite them into fellowship.** Help them connect with Christ and with His people.
3. **Recognize that every believer is a bridge.** You are a living connection between a lost world and the love of God. Don't underestimate your role.

WE PROCLAIM THE JOY FOR ETERNITY (1:4)

Did you catch that? Joy isn't complete until the message is shared and others join the fellowship. In the Christian life, joy grows when we give it away.

What is joy?

- **John 15:11** – "These things I have spoken to you, that my joy may be in you, and that your joy may be full."
- **Habakkuk 3:17–18** – "Even when crops fail and there's no food, "yet I will rejoice in the Lord."

Joy can bring happiness, but it is not the same as happiness. Happiness is circumstantial, but joy is relational and spiritual.

Happiness depends on what's *happening* around us. It's tied to good news, good food, good health, or good times. When things go well, we feel happy, but happiness fades when life falls apart. On the other hand, Biblical joy is rooted not in circumstances but in Christ. It comes from knowing God, being saved by grace, and trusting His presence no matter what we face.

Happiness rarely survives hardship—it's based on comfort. Joy can deepen *through* suffering because it is sustained by hope in God's character and promises.

Happiness comes and goes. It is a feeling that flickers with moods, seasons, or events. Joy in Christ is enduring—it starts now and continues forever because it's tied to eternal life and the presence of God.

Psalm 16:11 – "In your presence there is fullness of joy; at your right hand are pleasures forevermore."

"Happiness is like the weather—changing all the time. Joy is like the sun—it's always there, even when clouds hide it."

Why does this matter? It helps us keep a steady faith in unstable seasons. It keeps us from chasing false joys. It reminds us that Christ offers not surface-level cheer but deep, soul-satisfying, unshakable joy.

Three points of application:

1. **Let your joy in Christ be the fuel for your witness.** People are drawn to real joy—not hype, not performance, but authentic delight in Christ.
2. **Celebrate every step someone takes toward Jesus.** Rejoice when someone visits the church, asks a spiritual question, or begins reading the Bible. That's joy in motion.
3. **Never underestimate the ripple effect of your witness.** One conversation, one invitation, one prayer—you never know how God might use it to bring joy to someone else.

When Hudson Taylor was director of the China Inland Mission, he often interviewed candidates for the mission field. On one occasion, he met with a group of applicants to determine their motivations for service. "And why do you wish to go as a foreign missionary?" he asked one. "I want to go because Christ has commanded us to go into all the world and preach the gospel to every creature," was the reply. Another said, "I want to go because millions are perishing without Christ." Others gave different answers. Then Hudson Taylor said, "All of these motives, however good, will fail you during testing, trials, tribulations, and possible death. There is but one motive that will sustain you in trial and testing, namely, the love of Christ".

Who is one person you can tell this week about the Jesus you know?

Not to win an argument— Not to check a box— But to invite them into fellowship—with you, with Christ, and into the joy of the gospel.

2

1 John 1:5-10

Years ago, an hour south of Chattanooga, around 9 PM on a Sunday, the "Check Engine" light on the dashboard of my old Saturn began to blaze in its bright red glow. I knew there was trouble ahead. We stopped and looked under the hood, and then finished our trip.

As alarming as that light may be, we would all benefit from a spiritual "Check Engine" light. It is too easy for believers to ignore the signs and continue into a season of sin and backsliding away from God. We cannot experience true fellowship with God while deceiving ourselves about sin—honesty is the only way to walk in the light.

The Danger of Deception
1 John 1:5–10

After a brief introduction, John wades deep into the primary purposes of his letter. As a godly pastor, he can both encourage and admonish us in the same passage. He does not want to break the spirit of this young church, but he also cannot allow heresy to go unchecked. If we walk right with God, we must walk honestly with God—and ourselves.

We need to recognize three realities to avoid the temptation to sin...

A TRUTH: God is Light (v.5)

Notice that John talks about God before he talks about us. When we WANT to do better, we must remember it BEGINS with God. He is both the goal, the motive, and the power

In his writings, John makes three singular statements regarding God. He says God is spirit (John 4:24), God is love (1 Jn 4:8), and God is light (1:5). With these three simple statements, John is seeking to clarify for us the nature of God.

"God is light" carries a few implications.

The first implication is MORAL—God is good. Nahum 1:7. The Lord is good, a stronghold in the day of trouble; he knows those who take refuge in him. In a fallen world where we can question everyone's motives about everything that happens, we can be assured that God's motives are righteous and holy.

A second implication is CHARACTER—God is true. Deuteronomy 32:4. The Rock, his work is perfect, for all his ways are justice. A God of faithfulness and without iniquity, just and upright is he.

The third implication is SPIRITUAL—God is holy and righteous. Psalm 145:7; 17 They shall pour forth the fame of your abundant goodness and shall sing aloud of your righteousness... The Lord is righteous in all his ways and kind in all his works.

Why do John and others like Isaiah use light as a metaphor? *Consider the contrast between light and darkness.* Darkness is the absence of light. In Scripture, it often symbolizes sin, ignorance, evil, and separation from God. It represents life apart from His truth and presence—where people stumble, hide, or are blind to reality. To walk in darkness means to live in disobedience and self-deception, cut off from God's holiness and grace.

The implication is we are either walking in the light—where things are exposed—or in darkness, where things are hidden. King David turned from the light of God's holy love and plunged himself into the darkness of sin when he sent for Bathsheba. He believed the lie of his lust—it wouldn't matter, no one would know, the pleasure is worth the pain. Those who would walk with God must walk in the light as He is in the light

A PROBLEM: Man is a Sinner (v.6, 8, 10)

Even the believer struggles with temptation and sin. The sinful nature is defeated but remains in residence. It no longer commands, but it can cajole. Sin cannot tell us, but it can tempt us.

In three verses, John addresses our inadequate responses to the problem of sin in our lives. No believer WANTS to admit he is a sinner, but it is vital to our fellowship with God.

Listen to the personal struggle that Apostle Paul describes in Romans 7:15, 18, 24-25a

- For I do not understand my own actions. For I do not do what I want, but I do the very thing I hate.
- For I know that nothing good dwells in me, that is, in my flesh. For I have the desire to do what is right, but not the ability to carry it out.
- Wretched man that I am! Who will deliver me from this body of death? Thanks be to God through Jesus Christ our Lord!

So, let us not deny the struggle every believer faces. Let us recognize our self-deception.

John gives three false claims people make:

Claiming to know God while living in sin (v.6): "If we say we have fellowship with Him while we walk in darkness, we lie and do not practice the truth." This person talks the talk but doesn't walk the walk. They live in sin and pretend they are in fellowship with God. Others can see the lack of growth and maturity in our lives.

Claiming to have no sin nature (v.8), "If we say we have no sin, we deceive ourselves..." This is self-deception—pretending we're not fallen, not in need of grace. It denies that sin still dwells in us, even as believers. Others can see our disregard for righteousness

Claiming to have never sinned (v.10), "If we say we have not sinned, we make Him a liar..." This is an outright rejection of truth and calls God a liar. Others can see our denial of reality.

Tim Keller said, "The human heart is an idol factory, and we often can't see what we're worshiping because we've convinced ourselves it's something else."

Self-deception is one of the quiet but dangerous battles we all face. It occurs when we hide or deny the truth from ourselves—often without realizing it—to protect our desires or self-image. Instead of facing what's hard or uncomfortable, we suppress it. Scripture frequently uses the phrase "hardening the heart" to describe what happens when someone resists God's truth. While it may seem like a form of self-protection, it ultimately creates an inner conflict: deep down, we may sense the truth but choose not to admit it.

Galatians 6:7-8 Do not be deceived: God is not mocked, for whatever one sows, that will he also reap. For the one who sows to his own flesh will from the flesh reap corruption, but the one who sows to the Spirit will from the Spirit reap eternal life.

A PROMISE: Forgiveness is Available (v.7, 9)

John tells us two things that provide an eternity of hope and encouragement: "If we walk in the light... the blood of Jesus cleanses us..." (1:7) and "If we confess our sins, He is faithful and just to forgive..." (1:9)

Walk in the Light (1:7)

To "walk in the light" means living in the full exposure of God's truth and presence. It's not a call to live perfectly but to live honestly.

God already knows our hearts—He sees the thoughts we suppress and the sins we try to hide.

Walking in the light is a decision to stop hiding.

This kind of transparency brings freedom. It releases us from the burden of pretending. It nurtures true fellowship—not only with God but with other believers.

When we live openly before God, we become safe people to walk alongside. Christian fellowship cannot flourish in the shadows of secrecy or image management.

Confess Your Sin (1:9) *This is one of the most hope-filled promises in all of Scripture.*

God is **faithful**—He never turns away a repentant heart. When we confess, He receives us with mercy, not rejection.

God is **just**—His forgiveness is not based on leniency but on the finished work of Christ. That's why forgiveness is not just available—it's guaranteed for all in Christ.

God also **cleanses**—He doesn't just pardon the offense; He washes away the guilt and restores us to fellowship. Confession is not a shameful act—it's the doorway back to joy, freedom, and intimacy with God.

Self-deception is subtle and deadly. It leads us away from God and cuts us off from the joy of true fellowship. But when we walk in the light—honestly, humbly, and confessing our sins—we find that God is ready to forgive, cleanse, and restore.

Invite the Holy Spirit to examine your heart regularly. Let God's light reveal what needs to change. Practice honest confession, not just when you "feel bad," but as a lifestyle. Develop a rhythm of confession in prayer. Encourage honesty and grace in your Christian relationships. Cultivate environments where people can be honest about their struggles.

3

1 John 2:1-2

I knew an underwriting manager at The Prudential Insurance Company who was passionate about old cars. He would purchase an old car, such as an early model Ford Mustang that was in disrepair, and begin the slow process of restoring it to its original glory.

He first took the car apart—engine, body, and interior—and evaluated every component. He repaired what he could, and he replaced other parts as needed. He wanted everything to match the original version of the car, including the paint colors.

Believers can fall into disrepair. That is a nice way of saying, "Believers get out of God's will and into sin." When that happens, we need the Lord to restore us.

John addresses the reality of sin in the life of a believer in chapter one. Now he turns his attention to how God addresses that sin. He seeks to inform us of what provision God makes for sinning saints.

BELIEVER RESTORATION

1 John 2:1-2

In two short verses, John comforted struggling believers with the truth that Jesus intercedes when they sin. His words remain true. When you stumble, Jesus faithfully intercedes and restores you through His righteousness.

Let's consider three truths about the restoration available for sinners...

WE WILL STRUGGLE WITH SIN (2:1)

"My little children, I am writing these things to you so that you may not sin..."

Druid City Hospital in Tuscaloosa, Alabama, sits on a hill. The parking garage sits at the bottom of the hill. A stairway out of the garage leads to the hospital's front entrance. At the base of the garage staircase, nurses, technicians, orderlies, and even a few doctors were always gathered to smoke a cigarette. *It always seemed odd* that those who knew better than anyone else the dangers of smoking would be addicted to the practice.

Believers should not sin, but we do. We do not *have* to sin. There are times when we do not *want* to, but we do. Notice the care in John's voice. He has called us to be honest about sin in chapter one. It is a reality that we cannot deny.

We define sin as any failure to conform to God's holy character and law, whether in our actions, attitudes, or very nature. It includes doing what God forbids (sins of commission) and failing to do what God commands (sins of omission). Sin is rebellion against God, a corruption of what is good, and a falling short of the glory of God (Romans 3:23).

That definition points to several biblical words that describe how sin manifests itself: missing the mark, rebellion, corruption, and trespassing—the variations in our sin call for a broad array of words to describe it.

Sadly, we will struggle with sin while we live in this flesh. Even believers struggle with temptation. The Lord redeems our souls at salvation, but our flesh has to wait. The Scriptures say, "[We] ourselves, who have the first fruits of the Spirit, groan inwardly as we wait eagerly for adoption as sons, **the redemption of our bodies. For in this hope we were saved."** (Romans 8:23-24)

We *were saved spiritually* when we were justified before God because of Jesus' death, burial, and resurrection. We *will be saved physically* when we are gathered to God by Jesus at our death or His 2nd Coming.

- This is how Abraham can be a friend of God and fall into sin
- This is how Sampson can be the Judge who brings liberty to God's people, and fall into sin
- This is how King David can be a man after God's own heart, and fall into sin

We sin, but we do not want to. We sin, but we do not have to. This is what makes sin so tragic for believers.

Honesty is the first chapter in the book of wisdom. ~Thomas Jefferson.

If you would be restored from sin, it begins with honesty. You have sinned, which necessitates the restoration. Do not deny your sin: God calls you to pursue holiness. Do not surrender to sin: Engage in Scripture, prayer, and accountability to strengthen your walk. Do not despair over sin: God provides grace when you fall.

WE ARE NOT CONDEMNED BY SIN (2:1)

"...But if anyone does sin..."

One writer pointed out that John doesn't say "when" in a fatalistic sense, but "if" in a realistic sense. Sin is not the goal but a reality, even for believers. This phrase introduces hope: God has made provision for our failures.

Ask yourself this question: When am I most likely to sin? Is there a person, place, or circumstance that leaves me susceptible?

Consider King David. He fell into sin with Bathsheba. There is a method to his backsliding that left him susceptible to the temptation and eventual sin.

STEP ONE: Denying the Problem. David would not acknowledge that his lust led him. He ignored God's plan of one man and one woman for life. He had multiple wives and concubines.

STEP TWO: Ignoring the Escape. He ignored the staircase that would move him away from the temptation of Bathsheba. He hardened his heart when temptation buffeted him.

STEP THREE: Failing to Make a Plan. He did not care about trusting or glorifying God. He plotted for his pleasures.

STEP FOUR: Isolating from Accountability. David had no one he would allow to speak truth into his life. He had no accountability partner.

David fell into sin. He had to hear Nathan declare, "You are the man..."

There is hope. The Lord promises not to abandon His people. Many people consider Psalm 23 a song of death since we read it at funerals. It is actually a song of life. We have the promise that the Lord will restore His people.

Psalm 23:1-3 "The Lord is my shepherd; I shall not want. He makes me lie down in green pastures. He leads me beside still waters. He restores my soul. He leads me in paths of righteousness for his name's sake."

I always thought "restores my soul" meant that God mended broken hearts like a fisherman mending a net. It means, "to turn back." It is the work of a shepherd when a sheep wanders from the flock to find it and turn it back. A believer is not condemned again when he sins. He is pursued and restored by the Lord. "He restores my soul." It is a picture of repentance.

When you sin, do not hide from God; instead, run to Him. Confess quickly (1 John 1:9) and remember that you are still a child of God. Share with others his forgiveness, as other Christians need to hear that failure isn't final.

We Have Hope When We Sin (2:1c-2)

"...we have an Advocate with the Father—Jesus Christ the Righteous One. He is the propitiation for our sins..."

John encourages us with two words. One tells us what we have, the second tells us what He does.

WHAT WE HAVE IS AN ADVOCATE, someone who comes alongside to help or represent. Jesus doesn't excuse our sin; He pleads His righteousness on our behalf.

Perhaps a modern concept of the term would be a defense attorney. Although Satan prosecutes believers night and day before the Father due to sin (Rev. 12:10), Christ's High-Priestly ministry guarantees not only sympathy but also acquittal (Heb. 4:14-16).

WHAT HE DOES IS BEAR OUR PUNISHMENT. Propitiation means God fully expressed, appeased, and satisfied His wrath when it was poured out on Jesus when He hung on Calvary's cross.

How we consider punishment is an essential distinction between a believer sinning and a lost person. The lost person lives with the wrath of God upon them. The believer lives under the mercy of God. "For the whole world" means no one can stand before God and claim He made no sacrifice for them. Christ's offering is sufficient for all humanity.

Let's return once again to the example of the sinning saint, King David. Psalm 40 was likely written during the time of Absalom's rebellion. David's sin was the root of the problem, but he still had hope.

Psalm 40:1-4 I waited patiently for the Lord; he inclined to me and heard my cry. He drew me up from the pit of destruction, out of the miry bog, and set my feet upon a rock, making my steps secure. He put a new song in my mouth, a song of praise to our God. Many will see and fear, and put their trust in the Lord. Blessed is the man who makes the Lord his trust

Take comfort in Christ's advocacy—He stands for you even when you stumble. Approach God confidently in prayer (Hebrews 4:16)—you have a perfect representative. Live in freedom, not fear—your standing is secure because Jesus never fails.

There is hope for the stumbling saint.

Television is loaded with home restoration shows. The formula is simple: girl boss, interior designer wife, goofball construction husband. They help a young couple dive deep into debt with a house they cannot afford, needing massive repairs to make it livable.

Around 20 minutes into the show, a crisis arises that blows their budget apart just in time for a commercial. They return from the commercial, and we discover the compromise the team has arrived at.

I love it when they have the grand reveal. A big screen with a picture of the OLD house pulled apart to show the NEW house.

Here is the reveal for your restoration—JESUS

He is the one who restores, and He is the target of your transformation.

It is available through faith and repentance.

4

1 John 2:3-11

Susan says I am a coffee snob. She says I have raised three children who are coffee snobs. She probably anticipates me extending that to our grandchildren.

I do not like bad coffee.

If I am a coffee snob, she made that happen. She bought granola bars with a coffee flavor that I discovered was a collaboration with Caribou Coffee. I have always drunk coffee, but Caribou was the first to advertise "flavor notes." There was no turning back once I could identify the flavor notes I preferred.

When shopping for coffee, those "flavor notes" are the identifying marks of what I am seeking to enjoy.

This morning, we will consider two *marks of faith*—spiritual flavor notes—that the Lord expects every believer to display. These marks help us distinguish between true salvation and an emotional, religious experience.

Does your life display these marks of faith?

MARKS OF FAITH: Obedience and Love
1 John 2:3-11

The church at Ephesus was being pulled in two different directions. Some false teachers eloquently undermined Jesus, the Apostles, and the gospel of salvation. They are taking the philosophy of the day and substituting it for true faith and salvation. They are perverting the gospel.

This retired fisherman had also walked with Jesus and served them as a loving pastor and shepherd. The turmoil would have left the church confused. Without admonishing them, John seeks to encourage them. Like a kindly father, he tells them they know they are genuinely saved.

Let's consider the marks of biblical faith...

THE MARK OF OBEDIENCE (1 John 2:3-6)

John immediately gets to the point in verse 3: "And by this we know that we have come to know Him, if we keep His commandments."

Let's consider two crucial words in this verse that drive our interpretation. "KNOW" is used twice. The first time, it was just intellectual understanding. The second usage is about a deep, experiential relationship. John says, *"Here is how you can have assurance day by day that you know Him, that you are saved: look to His perfect work of atonement AND ongoing advocacy on your behalf... and keep His commands."*

The second word to consider is "KEEPING." This conveys the idea of guarding. We should guard God's commands as a precious treasure. And as we do, the treasure of our assurance is strengthened.

Obedience is not a condition *FOR* knowing God, but as clear evidence *OF* knowing God. It is not a burden but a blessing

Chuck Colson wrote, "To know God and to love God is intimately wed... and both lead to obedience". Jesus said, "If you love me, you will obey what I command" (John 14:15). John wrote, "This is the love of God, that we keep his commandments" (1 John 5:3). When we truly know Jesus, we delight in obeying Him.

The Stark Contrast: Saying vs. Doing

John draws a clear distinction between merely saying and actually knowing that Jesus is doing His will. Verse 4 gives the negative: "He who says 'I have known Him,' and does not keep His commandments is a liar, and the truth is not in him." This is not just a casual error; it's a fundamental deception. Such a person claims to have an authentic relationship with God but doesn't. Their disobedience exposes the deception in their claim. The truth is absent from their life.

Obedience Leads to Maturing Love and Abiding in Christ

Verse 5 shows the positive side: *"And whoever keeps His word, in him truly the love of God is perfected."* John links knowing, loving, and obeying God as a perfect triad of proof.

Verse 6 takes this further: *"He who says he abides in Him ought to walk in the same way He walked."* Abiding/remaining in Christ is the natural outgrowth of knowing Him. Jesus spoke extensively on this in John 15, emphasizing that apart from remaining in Him (the Vine), we can do nothing and will not produce fruit.

Faithful obedience to the WORD and WILL of God is non-negotiable for the believer!

In Homer's *Odyssey*, Odysseus must sail past the island of the Sirens—creatures whose beautiful songs lure sailors to shipwrecks. Forewarned,

Odysseus instructs his crew to plug their ears with wax and tie him to the mast, no matter how desperately he begs to be released. As they pass the island, the Sirens sing, and Odysseus is overwhelmed with a desire to follow their voice. He shouts for release, but the crew, obeying his earlier command, keeps rowing. Because they followed the plan, the ship passed safely, and they survived the danger.

Odysseus was saved not by his strength but by trusting wise instruction and relying on the obedience of his crew. In the same way, our spiritual safety doesn't come from willpower alone but from obeying God's Word—even when temptation calls loudly. Obedience is for God's glory and your good.

THE MARK OF FELLOWSHIP (1 John 2:7-11)

John now focuses on a specific command: the command to love. He calls this command both "old" and "new." The command is old since it has ancient roots in the law of Moses (*"love your neighbor as yourself,"* Lev. 19:18). We can also consider it new since it is finally fully realized in Jesus, who displayed it like never before. It is new and genuine in believers who walk as Jesus walked.

Love and Light Go Together; Hate and Darkness Reveal

John uses stark contrasts. He uses his "the one who says" statements to distinguish those in the light from those in the darkness. In verse nine, he says, "Whoever says he is in the light and hates his brother is still in the darkness." Love/hate reveals our actual spiritual state.

Verse 10 provides the contrast: *"Whoever loves his brother abides in the light, and in him is no cause for stumbling."* Consistently loving others gives evidence of having the life of God. It's a sign that you continually abide in the light. John equates loving our brothers and sisters with living in the light. Since "God is light" (1:5) and "God is love" (4:16), it's not surprising that love and light go together in the very person of God.

WHAT KIND OF LOVE? John's definition of love isn't weak or sentimental. It's a real, self-sacrificial commitment modeled on Jesus laying down His life for us. It is shown not just with words but with actions and in truth. Biblical love involves choosing the interests of the other over our own.

We Cannot Separate Our Love for God and Love for Others

In verse 5, John spoke of our love FOR GOD being perfected. In verses 7-11, the focus is on love FOR OTHERS. God's love received is redemption. God's love expressed is fellowship.

In The Return of the King, Frodo is overwhelmed by the burden of carrying the One Ring to Mount Doom. Exhausted, broken, and ready to give up, he collapses on the mountainside.

That's when Samwise Gamgee steps in. He can't carry the Ring for Frodo, but he says, "I can carry you!" and lifts Frodo onto his back to finish the journey.

Sam's love wasn't passive—it was sacrificial and faithful. He kept Frodo's mission alive. That's the essence of Christian fellowship: authentic love that lifts up the weary, walks alongside the burdened, and brings warmth to those whose spiritual fire is fading.

MARKS ON DISPLAY

Several years ago, I had lunch with a young pastor who had recently been installed as the new pastor of a local church. He shared that the first change he made from the previous pastor was to exit the green room. I didn't understand, so he explained that the church had a "green room" like a television talk show, where guests sat until they were to walk out on stage. The former pastor sat in a room off-stage until he was "on." I said it wasn't the most superficial, narcissistic misunderstanding of the nature of corporate worship I had ever heard of, but it would certainly be added to my list.

The American church is choking itself by pursuing superficial carnal approaches to ministry, worship, and "discipleship." We are imitating the world to attract the world while ignoring God's strategy for health and growth. Love and obedience are significant components of how God provides for the health of His church.

Acts 2:42-47 And they **devoted themselves to the apostles' teaching and the fellowship,** to the breaking of bread and the prayers. And awe came upon every soul, and many wonders and signs were being done through the apostles. And all who believed were together and had all things in common. And they were selling their possessions and belongings and distributing the proceeds to all, as any had need. And day by day, attending the temple together and breaking bread in their homes, they received their food with glad and generous hearts, praising God and having favor with all the people. **And the Lord added to their number day by day those who were being saved.**

OBEDIENCE is not a burden. It declares love for the Lord and commitment to the gospel. If we believe it, we will live it!

FELLOWSHIP is not superficial. It is a display of love for the Lord and His people. If we love Him, we will live it!

Remember, the main issue John has been addressing is the false idea that salvation is a kind of "secret knowledge." He is pushing back against the claim that someone can be truly saved by intellectual belief alone, without any real change in how they live. Scripture gives us these marks to provide assurance, not to create doubt.

5

1 John 2:12-17

A camera computer tries to find grey. The computer identifies the brightest and darkest points in the picture and seeks to balance these extremes with a midpoint, which is grey.

We live in a world of sin and righteousness, genuine and counterfeit, black and white. Too many professing believers behave as though grey is an option. It is a lie that cannot be sustained for long.

John writes one of his strongest admonitions to a young church bombarded by false teachers who are adopting the philosophy of the world and attempting to pass it off as the gospel.

In our passage today, we will see that John warned believers that love for the world leads to rebellion against God

Dangers of Worldliness
1 John 2:15-17

I encourage you to guard your hearts against worldliness so you can live faithfully to God.

Let's consider 3 dangers we face when we choose the world over the Lord...

WE FACE THE DANGER OF FORSAKING THE LOVE OF GOD (2:15)

As you read the passage, you recognize the train of thought John is leading us with in his words. He begins here with an ADMONITION against the world and worldliness.

First, we need to understand what he means when he says, "the world." It is a word he uses six times in these three verses.

In John's writings, the term "world" (kosmos) primarily refers to human life and society alienated from God. Sometimes it denotes the physical creation and humanity. John *typically* uses it to describe a spiritual reality opposed to God's kingdom. This "world" is characterized by material focus, hostility to God's Spirit, and rejection of Jesus.

We live in a world that shaped itself without the influence of God's word and character. Paul tells us the world is one of the three great enemies we face: The devil, the world, and our flesh.

Since worldliness is a significant spiritual danger. It takes potentially good activities and uses them to seduce a person away from godliness.

- It often manifests as a preoccupation with wealth, inappropriate desire for success or status, or distortion of relationships for power or gratification.
- Worldliness can be more spiritually dangerous than overt sins because it can be rationalized.

To prioritize the pleasures of this world, we make a trade-off. We choose to FORSAKE the love of God. ***We do not lose the love of God***—His agape love is fixed. We deny it and live in opposition to His love.

Either one is a genuine Christian marked by love and obedience to God, or one is a non-Christian in rebellion against God, i.e., in love with and enslaved by the satanically controlled world system. **~John McArthur**

One cannot love the world and live out their Christian faith. God's love is selfless and sacrificial. It is fixed upon the object of your affections regardless of their behavior.

- **The world is selfish.** That preoccupation with "self" destroys any authentic affection for others.

BUT WE TRY SO HARD TO HAVE BOTH IN OUR LIVES. We have a brown marble vanity in our bathrooms. A pale gecko got in and matched its color. It took a moment to see it when Susan called me into the room to catch and release it.

How much time do you spend seeking to "blend in?"

- You go to *work* or school, laugh at the jokes, consume the media, and sing their songs.
- You come to *church* and laugh at the jokes, consume the media, and sing our songs.

Your flirtation with the world demands a price be paid. You are abandoning God's work to shape you to Christ-likeness.

WE FACE THE DANGER OF FEEDING OUR DEADLY TEMPTATIONS (2:16)

John moves from the PROHIBITION to the CAUSE for his concern. John makes one statement but interrupts himself with examples. Let's consider the examples first.

The NATURE of our temptations.

John does not provide an exhaustive list, but he provides a range of categories.

These categories encompass the forms of temptation we face.

- ***The lust of the flesh*** relates to physical desires and doing wrong things, such as perverting good desires like thirst or intimacy into sinful acts.
- ***The lust of the eyes*** involves personal or self-centered desires. It is often linked to covetousness and selfishness.
- ***The pride of life*** concerns self-interests and being something one we shouldn't be, often associated with ambition and the desire to dominate others.

Remember, temptation is not sin—it is the enticement to sin. That enticement appeals to the needs God gives us but seeks to satisfy those needs in a manner forbidden by God.

The SOURCE of our temptations.

John assures us these temptations do not come from God. James speaks to this contrast.

James 1:13-17 Let no one say when he is tempted, "I am being tempted by God," for God cannot be tempted with evil, and he himself tempts no one. But each person is tempted when he is lured and enticed by his own desire. Then desire when it has conceived gives birth to sin, and sin when it is fully grown brings forth death. Do not be deceived, my beloved brothers. Every good gift and every perfect gift is from above, coming down from the Father of lights, with whom there is no variation or shadow due to change.

What a sad contrast. God gives FREELY what we need. We chase FRANTICALLY what we do not.

I have never been to a dog track to see the dogs race, but I have seen it on television. The greyhounds chase the bunny around the track. They can NEVER catch it because of the speed of the machine. The dogs would not be satisfied if the machine broke down and they caught up to it since the bunny is fake.

Do you see the sad contrast? God gives YOU freely what YOU need. YOU chase frantically what YOU don't need.

How do you overcome this craven temptation? Philippians 4:8. *"And now, dear brothers and sisters, one final thing. Fix your thoughts on what is true, and honorable, and right, and pure, and lovely, and admirable. Think about things that are excellent and worthy of praise."*

Fix your mind on the greatness of God and His blessings.

WE FACE THE DANGER OF SACRIFICING THE ETERNAL BLESSINGS (2:17)

John's train of thought finds its ultimate destination: the ADMONITION was followed by the REASONING now leads to the RESULTS.

This is the final assessment in the passage. This is the reality we are forced to confront and acknowledge.

> ***Dr Danny Akin says,*** "The heart of John's argument is now given. This final verse of the section, "contrasts the outcomes of these two loves, two lives, and two orientations toward Life." When compared with a life lived in the will of God, the things this life has to offer are really empty imitations of God's best. The things of the world seem to be of great value, but they are worthless when compared to the eternal blessings that come from doing the will of God. Jesus Christ in his death and resurrection has defeated the world that is opposed to God and has secured life eternal for those who believe."

John creates a wonderful word picture when he says, "the world is PASSING

AWAY." One use of this word in the first century had to do with the theaters of the day. At the conclusion of a scene, the curtain would come down, and the props would be picked up and moved offstage. In preparation for the next scene, new props would quickly be brought onstage.

John's point is that the world system opposed to God is like a scene in a play. When the scene comes to an end, the curtain falls and the props are removed.

The world system has a built-in design flaw—it is temporary. It is already on the way out.

On a recent vacation, Susan and I visited a market in Cozumel that sold designer handbags and backpacks. I have been carrying a Swiss Army backpack for 10 + years. It is rugged. It takes a beating and keeps going. I saw a bag from the same company being sold for 1/3rd the price of a bag in the States.

Then I picked up the bag. Immediately, I knew it was fake. It felt cheap and flimsy. If I dropped my laptop into the slot, it would likely rip the bottom out of the bag. The handle would not support the weight. It was a cheap imitation.

The reality that is worse than this man selling garbage is the fact that people were buying it, *most of the time*, knowing it was a knock-off. They wanted to pass it off as real.

- You live your life like that gecko trying to blend in with the world
- You live your life like that greyhound chasing what is not real
- You live your life trying to pass off a knock-off as the real thing.

Aren't you ready to stop?

6

1 John 2:18-27

Webster's Dictionary defines "apostasy" as an act of refusing to continue to follow, obey, or recognize a religious faith; abandonment of a previous loyalty. Sadly, we see apostasy all around us. The decline in the American church is evidence of apostasy. Many have abandoned their previous loyalty to the body of Christ.

In our passage, we will see John expose the way false teachers revealed their apostasy, abandoned Christ, and departed from His church. John warns us not just about *what* apostasy looks like, but *how* to avoid being swept into it.

Evidence of Apostasy
1 John 2:18-27

Don't be deceived—those who abandon Christ and His church expose a heart of spiritual rebellion.

Let's consider three words that give evidence of apostasy...

DENIAL: Apostasy Rejects the Biblical Jesus (vv. 18, 22–23)

John declares, "It is the last hour" - the entire church age between Christ's first and second advent. One of the characteristics of this period is opposition to Christ. We define those who seek to deny or degrade Jesus/gospel as "anti-Christs." Anti means both "against" and "instead of" Christ. These are not merely *opponents* but *substitutes* who offer alternative versions of Jesus. The apostates do not always reject religion—*typically,* they seek to corrupt it by presenting a different Jesus

THREE DENIALS OF JESUS

The Historical Denial. Some deny that Jesus of Nazareth was a real historical person. Others claim the Gospel accounts are entirely mythological constructions. Popular atheist arguments that Jesus is a fictional character. Some forms of secular humanism treat Jesus as pure legend.

The Messianic Denial. Denying Jesus is the promised Messiah of the Old Testament. Rejecting that Jesus fulfilled the prophetic promises about the coming Savior. Movements that acknowledge Jesus' existence but deny His unique role as God's anointed Savior.

The Trinitarian Denial. "Whoever denies the Son does not have the Father either" (v. 23). This reveals the inseparable unity of the Trinity. You cannot have a relationship with God the Father while rejecting God the Son. Unitarian theology that acknowledges God but rejects Christ's divinity. Interfaith movements that claim all religions worship the same God. Any attempt to maintain spirituality while abandoning Christ

Oprah Winfrey famously said she could not believe in a jealous God. She was fine with a God of love and blessings, but rejected the biblical notion that God is jealous. This was the turning point when she began to abandon the biblical narrative of Jesus/God/humanity and salvation.

False views of Jesus are not harmless; eternity is at stake. There is no salvation apart from the biblical Christ.

Apostasy exposes spiritual pride. The apostate believes they know better than Scripture. They fashion a Jesus that fits their preferences rather than submitting to who He truly is. This reveals the same pride that led to Satan's fall.

Apostasy reveals the heart. It is fundamentally about authority. It demonstrates a heart that wants to determine truth rather than submit to it. The apostate becomes their ultimate authority.

DECEPTION: Apostasy Misleads Jesus' People (vv. 20, 26–27)

Misery loves company. The apostate is not satisfied to pervert or reject the truth on their own; they desire to lead others astray. They find their strength in being affirmed by others who agree with them.

Again, there is a contrast between the false and the true, the counterfeit and the real. The false teachers wanted to lead Christians astray in order to gain power over them and to conscript them into their own clique. That sort of empire-building still lies behind many of the divisions caused by false teaching today.

> The Greek word for DECIEVE YOU (2:26), or "LEAD... ASTRAY", from the verb planao, meaning 'to cause to wander.' The flourishing sects and cults of the late twentieth century have often gained impetus by deceiving and deluding uncertain Christians with their extravagant claims and clever theories. The remedy is not just 'Truth' as an absolute, out there. It is also the experience of that Truth inwardly.
> ***~David Jackman, "The Bible Speaks Today"***

They try to lead the faithful astray. They target immature or ungrounded believers. The Holy Spirit exposes their lies AND helps us discern truth. Truth does not evolve—it abides

Rob Bell planted a church in Grand Rapids, MN, at age 29. In a few short years, they purchased an old mall because the congregation grew to 10,000. He was once the #1 downloaded preacher on iTunes podcasts. His book ***"Love Wins"*** (2011) was a declaration of his apostasy from biblical truth. He rejected Penal Substitutionary Atonement, taught that hell is not eternal, and began preaching universalism.

He says, "Jesus is hidden in various cultures and every aspect of creation. Some people find him, and some don't. Some call him Jesus; some have too much baggage with Christianity, so they call him by a different name..." This is *"The Hero with a Thousand Faces"* view of Christ promoted by Joseph Campbell. Eventually, Bell left his church and became a "public theologian" and worked to develop a talk show to espouse his apostate views and lead others away from Jesus.

REASONS PEOPLE ARE SUSCEPTIBLE TO APOSTASY

Emotional and Psychological Factors Many people struggle with challenging aspects of traditional Christian doctrine, particularly teachings about hell, divine judgment, and human sinfulness.

Cultural Pressures Modern Western culture increasingly emphasizes individual autonomy, universal acceptance, and skepticism toward absolute truth claims.

Intellectual Challenges Some people genuinely struggle with theological questions about God's justice, the problem of evil, or biblical interpretation.

Pastoral Concerns Many are motivated by compassion - they find it difficult to accept that loving family members or friends who aren't Christians face eternal punishment.

DESERTION: Apostasy Abandons Jesus' Church (v. 19)

Notice three critical truths John points out in this single verse.

"They went out from us." The verb tense indicates a deliberate, decisive departure. This wasn't gradual drifting but intentional abandonment. They physically removed themselves from Christian fellowship and community.

"They were not of us." Their departure exposed what was always true about their hearts. They **never** possessed genuine saving faith despite appearances. External association with the church doesn't guarantee internal transformation.

Matthew 7:21-23, "Not everyone who says, "Lord, Lord" will enter the kingdom."

"For if they had been of us, they would have continued with us." True believers endure in faith and fellowship. Genuine conversion produces lasting commitment to Christ's people.

I was once asked how we can draw inactive members back to church. My answer was simple. We need to pursue them with evangelism. Treat them like a lost person needing Jesus. The idea of "inactive church membership" is not biblical. It is essentially a panacea that lulls people into a false sense of security when they have lost.

This issue matters because Christianity is inherently corporate, not just individual. We demonstrate our love for God through our love for His people. Abandoning the church often reflects abandoning Christ Himself

Are you in danger of apostasy? Pride precedes the fall. Apostates often become critical and divisive before leaving. They increasingly reject authority. They resist biblical teaching and church discipline. They eventually withdraw from meaningful Christian relationships

What are the warning signs of apostasy?

- Consistent criticism of church leadership and direction
- Isolation from fellowship and withdrawal from community life
- Doctrinal drift that moves away from biblical truth
- Attraction to alternative spiritualities or secular philosophies

Do not become as Demas, one of Paul's assistants, whom he spoke of in 2nd Timothy 4:9-10 when he says, *"Do your best to come to me soon. For Demas, in love with this present world, has deserted me and gone to Thessalonica..."*

7

1 John 2:28-3:3

The NFL season is upon us. It begins in March with the start of the league's new year. That leads to free agency and the draft to build the team. But that is not the goal. This leads to OTAs and training camp, but that is not the goal. This leads to preseason games, but that is not the goal. This leads to the regular season, but that is not the goal. Making the playoffs is not the ultimate goal, nor is playing in the Super Bowl. The goal is to win the trophy.

Players and coaches can become distracted by all of the smaller, intermediate goals between the beginning of the year and the Lombardi Trophy. Champions learn to keep focused and driven on the ultimate prize.

Believers, in the same manner, can become distracted by the daily grind and endless temptations. We can forget that one day Christ will return to gather us to himself. Our great challenge is to live ready. We are to prepare ourselves daily for the moment our Savior calls us to Himself, either through death or His second coming.

John urged believers to abide in Christ so they would be ready at His return.

Living for His Return
1st John 2:28-3:3

My desire for us echoes that of the Apostle. That desire is for us to live each day ready for the return of Jesus.

Let's consider four ways to live ready for Christ's return...

LIVE RIGHTEOUS (2:28-29, 3:3)

Beginning with the second verse, first, we consider the issue of righteousness, which may need to be explained. We can consider God's nature and character to be holy. Because of His holy nature, all that He does is *right*, straight, or true. His activities are righteous.

Speaking of humanity, the Bible says, "There are none that are righteous, no not one..." (Romans 3:23) So, when we are saved, the righteousness of Christ is imputed to us, and God receives us as righteous.

2:29 tells us that this practice of righteousness is evidence of our salvation. The opposite would be equally true; the absence of righteous acts is a sign that we have no salvation.

Notice in 2:28, John gives us a *directive* and shows the *result* it produces. First, we will consider the directive. We are to ABIDE in Jesus.

What does that mean? John uses the word 68 times: Gospel of John: 40 x; 1 John: 24 x; 2 John: 3 x; Revelation: 1 x

Abide means to remain, stay, dwell — continuing in fellowship with Christ. Not an occasional visit; it's a settled relationship. In John's writings, abiding involves faith, obedience, and love.

I have been abiding with my wife, Susan, for 34 years. She permeates every aspect of my life. Who she is shapes who I am. I am my own person, but my identity is intrinsically connected to her. It is the same with believers in Christ. The longer we live *with* Christ, the more we are shaped to be *like* Christ.

Second, we consider the result. We have confidence in contrast with shame or disgrace. For believers, the difference at Christ's coming will not be whether they are saved, but whether they have lived faithfully. This is a call to perseverance and holiness so that our meeting with Christ is filled with joy, not regret over wasted opportunities.

Notice in 3:3, he returns to this idea of holy and righteous. A believer seeks to mortify the sins of the flesh, not revel in them.

How to Abide

1. **Stay in His Word** (John 15:7) — His truth shapes our lives.
2. **Stay in Prayer** — communication deepens a relationship.
3. **Stay in Obedience** (John 15:10) — love proves itself through obedience.
4. **Stay in Fellowship** — the body of Christ strengthens perseverance.

If we live daily in fellowship with Jesus, His return will be a moment of joy, not dread.

LIVE CHANGED (3:1)

John is about to share a truth with the church that he believes is extraordinary. He begins this next section with a call to stop and SEE! The word "See" is a call to stop, look, and be amazed — like pointing out something so beautiful you do not want to miss it.

He tells us three things in this verse:

You Are Loved by the Father (3:1a) *"What kind of love"* — literally, "what foreign kind of love," meaning it's unlike anything in this world. This love is given, not earned — we didn't climb up to God; He stooped down to us. Stop often to marvel at God's love for you — it will keep your heart humble, grateful, and secure.

You Are Part of God's Family (3:1b) *"...that we should be called children of God; and so we are."* This isn't a metaphor — it's a real, relational status. In Christ, we're not just forgiven sinners; we are adopted sons and daughters with full rights and inheritance. Adoption in the ancient world was permanent — nothing could disown, or break, that legal bond. Let your family identity in Christ define you more than your past mistakes, earthly titles, or the world's opinion.

You Are Misunderstood by the World (3:1c) *"The reason why the world does not know us is that it did not know Him."* Our values, priorities, and loyalties now align with Christ, so we no longer fit the world's mold. If the world rejected Jesus, it should not surprise us that it may misunderstand or reject us. Opposition is not a sign that something's wrong with your faith — it's often a sign you're walking closely with Christ. Don't compromise your identity to gain the world's approval; you already have the Father's acceptance.

My friend Jason and his wife are adopting three children. They have served as foster parents for them for a few years. The oldest recently asked the case worker when she can start calling them mom and dad. Their protector and provider has become their parent.

Make Time to Marvel at God's Love. Begin each morning by thanking God specifically for ways you've experienced His love — even in small, ordinary mercies (sunrise, breath, forgiveness, peace in hardship).

Live Like a True Child of God. Approach God as a beloved son or daughter — not a stranger begging for scraps. Ask boldly and trust His fatherly heart.

When you feel defined by failure, success, or someone else's opinion, pause and say out loud: *"I am a child of God —"*

Endure the Struggle. Remember that following Christ may cost you popularity, opportunities, or comfort. Decide in advance that His approval is worth more than all of those.

LIVE EAGER (3:2)

This is my favorite verse in the passage. John's words are encouraging. The future the Lord plans for us SHOULD create a sense of eagerness amongst His people. Salvation began a process of transformation for us. Our souls are redeemed, and our lives are starting to change. The flesh awaits His return. Notice that John mentions his appearance twice in the verse. This is the source of our eagerness!

WE ARE EAGER FOR OUR CHANGE. *We are his children NOW, and what we will be has not yet appeared.*

We become frustrated by the world's oppression and our hearts' weakness. But Paul reminds us that the Lord is committed to completing the transformation of His people. Philippians 1:6 "And I am sure of this, that he who began a good work in you will bring it to completion at the day of Jesus Christ."

WE ARE EAGER FOR HIS RETURN

The language of scripture is essential. Jesus will be glorified *IN* His saints. His glory will shine *THROUGH* us who long to see Him return.

2 Thessalonians 1:7-10 "...when the Lord Jesus is revealed from heaven with his mighty angels in flaming fire, inflicting vengeance on those who do not know God and on those who do not obey the gospel of our Lord Jesus. They will suffer the punishment of eternal destruction, away from the presence of the Lord and from the glory of his might, when he comes on that day to be **glorified in his saints**, and to be marveled at among all who have believed, because our testimony to you was believed."

It may seem simplistic, but it is the truth. Jesus will gather us TO Himself at His second coming. He will also glorify Himself THROUGH us on that day.

Christian singer Wayne Watson put his heart's desire into words in his song, ONE DAY:

One day, Jesus will call my name
As the days go by, I hope I don't stay the same
I want to get so close to him that there is no big change
On that day that Jesus calls my name....

Are you eager for Christ's return?

For many of us, the fall is a season of joy as football returns.

This is also a season of dread. Storms form off the coast of Africa that make their way to North America as hurricanes. There is the lingering concern that those storms will bring destruction. For the believer, the anticipation of Jesus' return should be a season of joy.

Are you eager for Christ's return?

8

1 John 3:4-10

There is a phenomenon associated with the 9/11 attacks. It is called the 9/11 divorces. One such case came about when a married man skipped work to spend the day away from the office he had in one of the towers with his secret girlfriend.

When the towers were attacked, his wife feared for his life and began to call him to check on him. He had his cell phone turned off. He turned on his phone and saw all the missed calls, which he returned before seeing the news of the attacks on his office.

When he returned his wife's call, he lied that he had been in a meeting all morning. His ignorance of the danger and destruction revealed him to be a liar.

The word of God says much about our secret sin being made light:

- **Luke 12:2-3** – "Nothing is covered up that will not be revealed, or hidden that will not be known. Therefore, whatever you have said in the dark shall be heard in the light, and what you have whispered in private rooms shall be proclaimed on the housetops."
- **Galatians 6:7** – "Do not be deceived: God is not mocked, for whatever one

sows, that will he also reap."

God uncovers sin in His time, but sin uncovers the truth about us every day. Our actions and attitudes are the most unmistakable evidence of our salvation — or our lack of it. John explains that a life that pursues sin declares that they do not know Jesus.

EXPOSED BY SIN

1 John 3:4-10

Let's consider three types of sin that reveal the truth about our hearts...

WILLFUL SINS (3:4-5)

John addresses the reality of sin in the believer's life. Since we live in the flesh, *there will be times when we give in to sin.* But it should be the exception. Sin should not be the reputation or testimony of a follower of Jesus Christ.

Notice the language John employs: "Practice" is used six times in these seven verses. It is the Greek word "*poiema,*" which is also translated "to do" or "to work." Paul uses it in Ephesians 2:10 when he says believers are the Lord's "workmanship." John is pointing to sin that is not accidental or unintended.

To drive the nature of our failure, he employs another word, "lawless" in 3:4. There are several words and pictures used for "sin" in the Bible. Sin is weakness. (Romans 3:23) Sin is iniquity or corruption, pointing to its polluting effect. (Psalm 51:2) Sin is also lawlessness or rebellion. (Genesis 3)

> *[Lawlessness] unwillingness to comply with the guidance of authority, especially refusal to follow God's will. The first and most crucial act of disobedience occurred when Adam and Eve ate of the forbidden fruit (Genesis 3). Like all later human disobedience, that act involved setting the desire of the flesh above the will of God. As a result of this, all people*

became "sons of disobedience" (Ephesians 2:2) ~Nelson Illustrated Bible Dictionary

Lawlessness is not a temptation that catches us unprepared. This is intentional, willful sin. King David did not stumble into sin with Bathsheba. He saw her—sent servants to bring her to him—and then plotted the cover-up.

Notice in 3:5, John reminds us of the contrast. Believers identified with Jesus should reflect Jesus, who came to remove sin, not practice it.

It is to the shame of the believer to be found plotting and planning our sin. We may hide it from men, but we cannot hide it from God.

- **Numbers 32:23,** "...you have sinned against the Lord, and be sure your sin will find you out."
- **1st Timothy 5:24,** "The sins of some people are conspicuous, going before them to judgment, but the sins of others appear later."

If you are practicing your sin, you are either a backslidden believer or a deluded lost man who thinks he is alright. Either way, get right with God today before you are judged.

HABITUAL SINS (3:6-9)

Be wary of sin. What starts as a single compromise can quickly devolve into a habitual lifestyle.

The preachers of earlier generations were correct when they said, "Sin will take you further than you want to go, keep you longer than you want to stay, and cost you more than you want to pay."

Growing up, verse 6 scared me. I learned it in the King James translation. *"Whosoever abideth in him sinneth not: whosoever sinneth hath not seen him, neither known him."* I was always afraid that if I slipped up ONE time, I was bound for hell. I had not LOST my salvation; I had never had it in the first place.

With all due respect, that is a poor translation. The tenses of the verbs point to ongoing action, not a single, occasional event.

It appears Gnosticism was creeping into the church. Many false teachers in John's day claimed that sin didn't matter because the physical body was evil and only the spirit mattered.

John takes the problem of habitual sin and drives to the core issue. Your attitude towards sin reveals the disposition of your heart. John uses the language of family or origin to paint the picture. Those who abhor sin and seek to mortify it in their lives show they are the "children of God," or "born of God." Those who have no regard for righteousness are "of the devil." (3:8)

The language of the family takes the issue away from being merely academic. It helps us understand the matter with clarity. We know how "family resemblance" works.

I have two grandchildren. Jonathan recently told me that Thomas looks like the Hansons, but acts like Jonathan. Pippin looks like our family, the Dixons, but acts like Stephanie. Just as physical children resemble their parents, spiritual children reflect their spiritual father. A child may act up, but you can still see the resemblance to his parents. A man who claims God as Father but continually lives like the devil shows who he belongs to.

If you are practicing your sin, you are either a backslidden believer or a deluded lost man who thinks he is alright. Either way, get right with God today before you are judged.

How can I know? Consider the disposition of your heart.

- The believer confesses sin when he stumbles.
- The lost man excuses sin as if it doesn't matter.

APATHETIC SINS (3:10)

Verse 10 begins by reiterating the message that our attitude towards sin reveals our heart. Then John adds an interesting thought: how we care about fellow believers is a test.

Remember—"child of God" and "adopted" are not metaphorical ideas. Those phrases are reality for the believer. Christians are the children of God.

In the same manner, "brother and sister" in Christ is not a metaphorical idea. Christians are the family of faith.

Our goal is to have a relationship based upon love. It is love for God and love for each other. Consider what God's love amongst us reveals...

Love Reveals the New Birth

A newborn shares DNA with his parents. A Christian shares spiritual DNA with God, so His love must show up. God is love (4:8). If His life is in us, His love flows through us.

Love Reveals Our Union with Christ

John 13:35: "By this all people will know that you are my disciples, if you have love for one another." Our love for each other is **the visible badge of discipleship**.

Love Reveals the Spirit's Presence

Romans 5:5: "God's love has been poured into our hearts through the Holy Spirit." The Spirit implants a supernatural love that goes beyond personality, preference, or natural affection.

I called this the sin of apathy because believers are to have sincere affection for each other.

> *Apathy implies neglect; you just don't care. Hate is an active emotion in response to something that affects your life. I hate doing laundry. But, once per week, I suck it up and do the laundry. I get some form of satisfaction that I've conquered a hated task. Lately, I've fallen into* apathy, *largely due to the COVID-19 shutdown. I don't care about laundry. Since I am not going anywhere, I've settled into wearing the same style of yoga pants and t-shirts I have in abundance. I let my laundry pile up. I normally would feel disgusted at some point and just get it done. Now, as long as there's something to wear, I just don't care. A few times in the past 5 months, I've dragged a bag of t-shirts and yoga pants to the laundry, but didn't feel good afterward. It was just "yep, I've got clean t-shirts and yoga pants... the same stuff I was wearing a week ago, 2 months ago." No sense of accomplishment. I used to love to shop for clothes. Not now; what am I going to buy? T-shirts and yoga pants. Apathy is worse than hate in almost every situation. Hate can escalate and eventually solve a problem; apathy doesn't even acknowledge the problem, and everyone loses.* ***~Melissa Jeswald Quora.com***

The man who claims to love the Lord but is indifferent to the Lord's children is not a son of God. Where there is no concern for sin, there is no actual evidence of love for the holy God. John isn't saying Christians never sin. John is saying Christians can't *make peace* with sin. You can't love God and love your sin at the same time.

If you are practicing your sin—you are either a backslidden believer or a deluded lost man who thinks he is alright. Either way, get right with God today before you are judged.

9

1 John 3:11-18

An early 2000s movie called PROOF OF LIFE told the story of Terry Thorne, who negotiated the rescue of an American businessman in Central America kidnapped for ransom.

The movie was based on a Vanity Fair article, *Adventures in the Ransom Trade,* which told of dozens of wealthy people kidnapped every year. One of the negotiator's tactics is to demand "proof of life," so they know they are not wasting time and resources. This strategy keeps the victim relatively safe.

John frequently returns to the issue of "proof of life" for believers. He wants us to know, with certainty, that we have eternal life. The matter is important for two reasons. False teachers and life struggles can cause us to doubt. Spiritual pride can give us a false sense of hope.

Either way, we need to be certain of our salvation. John told this Ephesian congregation that ONE OF THE WAYS our salvation is made evident is by the love we have for each other.

PROOF OF LIFE

1 John 3:11-18

I pray that we would demonstrate our salvation by loving fellow believers through sacrificial actions, not just empty words.

Let's consider a few important elements of the passage:

JOHN GIVES US A COMMAND TO CONSIDER (3:11, 14)

John reminds us of Jesus' words regarding our salvation and the love we should have for one another.

John 13:34-35 A new commandment I give to you, that you love one another: just as I have loved you, you also are to love one another. By this all people will know that you are my disciples, if you have love for one another."

1 John 2:7-11 Beloved, I am writing you no new commandment, but an old commandment that you had from the beginning. The old commandment is the word that you have heard. At the same time, it is a new commandment that I am writing to you, which is true in him and in you, because the darkness is passing away and the true light is already shining. Whoever says he is in the light and hates his brother is still in darkness. Whoever loves his brother abides in the light, and in him there is no cause for stumbling. But whoever hates his brother is in the darkness and walks in the darkness, and does not know where he is going, because the darkness has blinded his eyes.

This is a new commandment, but it is not a new commandment. It is old in that we should ALWAYS love our brothers. We were commanded under the law to love, but it was powerless to compel love. It is new in that the Holy Spirit within us makes it possible.

So, John gives us a command to consider. We are to love each other. The question I must ask of myself is, "Do I?"?

JOHN GIVES US A CONTRAST TO CONSIDER (3:12-17)

John pulls forward an unlikely and extreme example of a heart devoid of love by calling our attention to Cain. This son of Adam and Eve murdered his own brother, Abel.

Genesis 4:2-5, 8 When they grew up, Abel became a shepherd, while Cain cultivated the ground. When it was time for the harvest, Cain presented some of his crops as a gift to the Lord. Abel also brought a gift—the best portions of the firstborn lambs from his flock. The Lord accepted Abel and his gift, but he did not accept Cain and his gift. This made Cain very angry, and he looked dejected... One day Cain suggested to his brother, "Let's go out into the fields." And while they were in the field, Cain attacked his brother, Abel, and killed him.

Notice that both Abel and his offering were accepted. Both Cain and his offering were rejected. It was both the gift and the giver that were scrutinized.

We consider that as an extreme example, but it is appropriate. We may recoil at being linked to murder, but it is appropriate. Jesus reminds us that a heart hardened towards others is a sin against God.

Matthew 5:21-22 "You have heard that it was said to those of old, 'You shall not murder; and whoever murders will be liable to judgment.' But I say to you that everyone who is angry with his brother will be liable to judgment; whoever insults his brother will be liable to the council; and whoever says, 'You fool!' will be liable to the hell of fire.

To degrade someone made in the image of God is a sin against God.

Craig Keener tells us Cain was a hero to some in the ancient world. Gnostics and Antinomians revered him because he disregarded the rules governing our behavior. Philo, an ancient Jewish philosopher in Alexandria, said Cain was a symbol of self-love

Such a contrast with Jesus. Cain is the embodiment of hate (3:15), and Jesus is the embodiment of love. Hate is negative. It seeks the other's harm. Hate leads to activities against another person. To rob someone of life is the greatest sin we can commit against them. Love is the positive. It seeks the other's good. Love leads to activities to benefit another person. To sacrifice on their behalf is the greatest expression of love for them.

JOHN GIVES US A CALLING TO CONSIDER (3:18)

Using the language of a loving shepherd, not a scolding judge, John teaches that authentic love is an active, not passive, force. Words without action are hypocrisy. Deeds without sincerity are empty. When love is both active and authentic, it reflects the love of Christ and gives evidence of our salvation.

In the second and third centuries, devastating plagues swept through the Roman Empire. Most people, including physicians, fled the cities to save themselves. But Christians stayed behind.

Historians like Dionysius of Alexandria recorded that believers nursed the sick, fed the hungry, and even buried the dead at risk to their own lives. Many Christians died as a result of caring for others. The pagan emperor Julian the Apostate, a critic of Christianity, complained in frustration that Christians were "advancing through the loving service rendered to strangers," and that "the godless Galileans support not only their poor but ours as well."

We need to remove adjectives when discussing love. Love is not active- authentic- selfless- sacrificial- it is ALL love, it is ONLY love. The only adjective we should consider is ABSENT love

HOW DO I LIVE THIS OUT?

3 Truths about love from this passage:

Love Forgives Quickly (v. 11, 15)

John contrasts love with Cain's hatred. Harboring bitterness is a form of spiritual murder. Forgiveness reflects the Father's love and shows the heart has been changed. When you forgive, you declare the gospel louder than your words.

Love Meets Needs Sacrificially (vv. 16–17)

Christ laid down His life — the ultimate act of love. We prove we are His children when we meet the needs of others. Love is costly — if it never costs me anything, it may not be real.

Love Encourages and Builds Up (v. 18)

Love is not empty talk — it strengthens others with truth, hope, and kindness. Barnabas, "the son of encouragement," stood by Paul when others doubted him. Encouragement fuels perseverance in the faith. A text, note, or kind word can be life-giving to a struggling believer

10

1 John 3:19-24

The drummer on America's Got Talent was almost silent on the television. He should have been at the forefront of the audio mix, but he was virtually silent. He was beating his drums ferociously. He looked like Animal, the drummer on The Muppet's television show.

As a preacher, I fear I can become like that drummer. I am beating the drum. I am pounding out the message, but it is getting lost in the sea of ideas that bombard us daily. We hear the Word preached, but we have already heard THAT sermon before.

Such is the challenge of this vital message from 1st John on the importance of love amongst the body of Christ.

John echoes his primary themes throughout the book. There are five tests of salvation given in the letter, and almost all of them are mentioned more than once. None of them is mentioned more than love for God and His church.

John speaks to the importance of love in every chapter

- We are to love and have fellowship with God and His church. (1:6-7)
- We are to show love for others. (2:7-11)

- We are to love one another. (3:11-15)
- We are to sacrifice for each other. (3:16-18)
- We are to love one another. (4:7)
- We cannot love God and hate our brother. (4:20)
- We are to display our love through our concern for our brothers' sins. (5:16)

It is a drum I have beaten repeatedly— love for God and each other is a drum we need to beat ferociously.

In this passage, John reaffirms the truth again, but points to the blessings of assurance love affords us.

BLESSINGS OF ASSURANCE
1 John 3:19-24

As we read this passage, we see a chain of blessings. One truth leads to another truth, which lays a foundation of assurance of the salvation we have found in Jesus.

"The Security of the Believer" and "The Assurance of Our Salvation" are similar but distinct.

- Security of the believer is the OBJECTIVE truth that we are saved based upon what God has done and continues to do for His church.
- Assurance of salvation is the SUBJECTIVE experience of confidence or conviction regarding our salvation based upon how we are growing in our faith.

Let's consider how love fuels the assurance every believer can experience...

Love Leads to Assurance (vv. 19–20)

Notice John connects our assurance with "truth." God's Word is true. Jesus is the truth. Our salvation is based upon the fixed revelation of God to men—prophets and apostles—transmitted to us via inspiration.

By loving in deed and truth (v. 18), *"we shall know that we are of the truth and reassure our hearts before him."*

When Satan and the world seek to undermine your faith, you can trust God's word, His presence, and His assurance. He is greater than the accusations. Even if our hearts condemn us, God's greater knowledge assures us. (3:20)

Point: Love is selfless and sacrificial! It proves we are truly God's children and calms our doubts.

Assurance Leads to Confidence (v. 21)

This is not a call for confidence from a callous heart. Often our hearts are hardened, and we can sin without conviction. This is the heart that humbly recognizes what God has been doing, and we trust His word about us.

"A heart at peace gives boldness before God." ~Anonymous

Love-driven obedience clears the conscience and opens the way for confidence in His presence.

Point: Love produces courage — no fear or shame in approaching God.

Confidence Leads to Answered Prayer (v. 22)

John brings together some truths that can trip up well-meaning believers. We go to the Lord and ask, but we do not always receive what we want. The Bible does say God will give you the desires of your heart... doesn't it? So, am I to assume I can ASK and God is obligated to provide?

A godly believer walking in faith, humility, and obedience has the assurance that the Father is working in his life. Therefore, his prayer life is vital as he seeks God's will. He prays, knowing the Father is shaping him into the image of Christ. The following verse from the Psalms points to the result of his prayers and includes a "qualifier."

Psalm 37:4 Delight yourself in the Lord, and He will give you the desires of your heart.

We read the phrase, "He will give you the desires of your heart," which can create a distorted image of God. He is not a cosmic Santa Claus waiting to dispatch toys, trinkets, and cash to us. The qualifier mentioned is the call to "*delight*" yourself in the Lord. This simple statement governs what we can expect in the answers to our prayers.

In short, God is not obligated to submit to our every whim. He is not obligated to give us whatever our hearts desire. When we pray, we seek His will for us. As we grow in our faith, our desires change. They become less self-focused and more Christ-focused.

John picks up on that and brings the prayer and the qualifier together. We receive when we walk in obedience and delight in Him. Prayer changes us! Obedience changes us.

As we pray for God's will, we see God's provisions. It emboldens us to seek God's face even more. We grow confident in our prayers.

Point: Love fuels obedience, obedience fuels prayer, and prayer brings blessing.

Obedience Leads to Fellowship (vv. 23–24a)

God's "commandment" is boiled down to two: believe in Christ and love one another. Keeping these commandments results in God abiding in us, and us in Him.

We have spoken much about fellowship and love within the body of Christ. The presence—or absence—of love amongst us is a bold commentary upon the nature of our salvation.

The truth is, the fellowship we have with each other is a byproduct of the fellowship we have with God.

The first casualty of Adam's sin in the Garden of Eden was his relationship with God. The second casualty was his relationship with Eve, his wife.

We cannot have a proper relationship with others till we have a proper relationship with God. If that primary relationship is healed through the blood of Jesus, we will be motivated to heal our relationships with others.

Point: Love proves our union with Christ.

Fellowship Leads to Assurance of the Spirit (v. 24b)

The Spirit confirms God's presence in us. Love and obedience aren't done in human strength, but in the Spirit's power.

Point: Love opens the door to a Spirit-given assurance that we belong to Him.

The Chain Summarized: Love → Assurance → Confidence → Answered Prayer → Fellowship → Spirit-given Assurance

John shows that authentic love is not just a duty; it's the foundation for a life full of confidence, prayer, and Spirit-filled assurance.

11

1 John 4:1-6

The history of the church is a history of Jesus being degraded.

622 AD Mohammad went out in the desert and returned with an inaccurate view of God. He said Jesus was a prophet—only a prophet. He degraded the Son of God.

In 1829, Joseph Smith claimed that an angel named Moroni led him to tablets containing a revelation from God. He said Jesus is God, but a lesser God. He degraded the Son of God.

In the 1870s, Charles Taze Russell founded the Jehovah's Witnesses with the claim to have a better translation of the bible. This new translation degrades Jesus. He degraded the Son of God.

And the list continues over and over again—L. Ron Hubbard, Mary Baker Eddy, and others.

The truth of the gospel is constantly being questioned. The identity of Jesus is under assault, and the church is the battleground where the war is waged.

In this age of political correctness, unhinged tolerance, and unity at any cost, it seems mean and outdated to tell someone that they are wrong. However, Scripture lets us know that the best thing we can do for someone is to speak and live the truth, regardless of how others react. We may change our methods, but we cannot compromise on our message.

John tells us that we can pass the ***test of truth*** if we keep biblical Jesus at the forefront of our lives.

CHRIST UNDER ASSAULT

1 John 4:1-6

Let's consider the ways believers can pass the test of truth...

WALK IN DISCERNMENT (1)

The early church faced a dilemma. They were attracting people with corrupt motives, and they were losing people with weak commitments.

The corrupt motives were those of the false teachers who wanted to co-opt the churches for their own selfish reasons. The two primary motives of the false teacher are ego (Jude 4) and money (1 Tim 6:3-5).

The weak commitments were those of the members who wanted the blessings of fellowship but did not have to face the obstacles to devotion. (2:19)

The false teachers attempted to gain a following by synthesizing their carnal philosophy with biblical language and terms. To gain an audience, they needed to *disqualify* the apostles and *degrade* the savior.

The church at Colossae faced the same problem. Paul wrote to them and said, "See to it that no one takes you captive by philosophy and empty deceit, according to human tradition, according to the elemental spirits of the world, and not according to Christ." (Colossians 2:8)

The identity of Jesus is under attack, and the church is the battleground where the war is waged.

There is a philosophy that appeals to us since it arises from the flesh and satisfies our pride. Because of that, we must be wary—we must scrutinize every message and messenger. The world has not changed in 2,000 years; we have just improved our means of transmitting the messages.

Consider some examples of the CORRUPTED PHILOSOPHY of the world:

- **Truth is Relative.** "My truth may not be your truth." Truth is that which accords with reality. To deny this is to render all contracts, property ownership, and personal relationships moot.
- **Love is Love.** "The heart wants what the heart wants." In reality, there is a limit on who and how we can express our attractions.
- **Religious Ecumenicalism.** "All religions basically teach the same thing." The truth is, there are distinct differences between faith traditions.

To combat this corruption of truth, we must apply discernment.

Discernment is the ability to understand what is difficult to see. It involves knowing how to tell what is valuable from what is not, especially in spiritual or moral areas. It is closely linked to wisdom and the skill to see and understand people, things, or situations clearly and wisely. In a biblical sense, spiritual discernment is described as the ability to tell the difference between truth and error, which is essential for wisdom.

This is not a judgment that involves condemning a person. Discernment is concerned with evaluating output and outcomes.

Judgment considers the ROOT, and discernment considers the FRUIT.

Judgment considers the REASONS, and discernment considers the RESULTS.

Discernment in action is opening the milk carton and taking a sniff. This is not a condemnation of the dairy industry; it is simply a verification of what you have in your refrigerator. When they degrade Jesus, it is of the Devil.

FOCUS ON JESUS (2-3)

Notice "spirit" is almost always lowercase in these verses: "every *spirit* that confesses; every *spirit* that does not confess..." It can be that John is discussing the attitude of the person. It is equally true that he means a fallen angel, a demon. Actually, I believe it is both. A demon who knows the truth can encourage you to question the truth. The truth of the gospel they question, related to Jesus, is the incarnation of God in the flesh.

There are countless reasons why the doctrine of the incarnation is essential. Let me share one that should be of great interest to us. Salvation requires a true God-Man to be valid.

- As a man, Jesus could stand in humanity's place, obeying where Adam failed and dying for human sin.
- As God, His sacrifice has infinite worth, sufficient to atone for the sins of the world.
- If Jesus were only a man, His death would have no saving power.
- If He were only God, He could not represent us. Only the God-Man could be our Savior (1 Tim. 2:5).

So, Satan, the World, and our very flesh attack the incarnation to degrade Jesus. Again, *the identity of Jesus is under attack, and the church is the battleground where the war is waged.*

There continue to be two major ways the spirit of antichrist attacks Jesus

DENY JESUS. They deny his existence by saying he is only human, a myth, or a legend. They deny his uniqueness by saying he was not born of a virgin nor resurrected after His death.

DEGRADE JESUS. They degrade Him by saying Jesus was a wise philosopher. This strips Him of His authority to save, leaving only moralism without the gospel. They degrade Him by saying say Jesus was a political revolutionary. This confines His mission to earthly justice, neglecting His work of redemption from sin. They degrade Him by promoting the "Good Vibes" Jesus. In popular spirituality, Jesus is portrayed as a cosmic life coach or positivity guru. This ignores His holiness, His call to repentance, and His lordship over all.

LISTEN TO GOD (4-6)

John returns to a favorite title for his church—"Little Children." He is addressing them as a gracious parent. These are not words of reproach, but of loving encouragement. He begins with a declaration and makes a telling distinction. Let's consider the distinction first.

DISTINCTION OF SOURCE (4:5-6)

This is the division he has already mentioned. The false gospel has an attraction to those of the world since it is an appeal to the flesh. Those who are of God recognize the ministry of the apostles and the inspiration of the scriptures.

His Word is our guide. His Word is the tool of evaluation. **Psalm 119:105** Your word is a lamp to guide my feet and a light for my path.

DECLARATION OF SUCCESS (4:4)

With all this in mind, John comforts his people—You can resist the lie. You have overcome the lie because you are His. You have overcome the lie because He is greater than them

Our success and victory are not because we win. Victory is not because we "declare" it. Victory is won by the one who defeated the grave. The power of the gospel is the power of creation. The power of the gospel is the power of the resurrection. The application of the power is seen in a young man who walked into a valley to face a giant with nothing but a sling.

Why was David successful? Consider his motivation, "That all the earth may know that there is a God in Israel." (1 Sam 17:46) He fought for the glory of God.

I am reminded that the church was attracting people with corrupt motives, and they were losing people with weak commitments.

Weak commitments are evidence that we do not understand the power and presence of God.

Come, Thou Fount of every blessing,
Tune my heart to sing Thy grace;
Streams of mercy, never ceasing,
Call for songs of loudest praise.
Jesus sought me when a stranger,
Wand'ring from the face of God;
He, to save my soul from danger,
Interposed His precious blood.

Prone to wander, Lord, I feel it;
Prone to leave the God I love:
Take my heart, oh, take and seal it
With Thy Spirit from above.
Rescued thus from sin and danger,
Purchased by the Savior's blood,
May I walk on earth a stranger,
As a son and heir of God.

12

1 John 4:7-12

When I open the medicine cabinet, I never know exactly what to take. We buy generic painkillers, and I recognize Tylenol and Advil. I get confused between acetaminophen and ibuprofen. Those ingredients are the actual medicine because they are the active ingredients. Everything else in the capsule is just a filler or binder and doesn't affect our pain.

Life is full of fillers. There are activities we pursue that help us "hold it all together," but do not have lasting value. Consider the pain and misery in this world—even in your own life—and ask, "What is the active ingredient that can bring real change?" ***John says that salvation is the product of God's active love.***

John connects our mutual affection within the body of Christ to the very nature of God and His love-motivated activities in Christ. ~John Stott

GOD'S ACTIVE LOVE

1 John 4:7–12

Let's consider the elements of God's active love

GOD'S ACTIVE LOVE REVEALS (V. 7–8)

This refrain of "love one another" echoes through the passage: It serves as an exhortation. (4:7) It acts as a call to duty since John states, *"we also ought to love one another."* (4:11) And it functions as a hypothesis, *"If we love one another."* (4:12)

Brotherly love and mutual affection flow from God's eternal nature. In this letter, John mentions love 46 times, with 27 references in 4:7-21. All 27 times, he uses the word "agape." It is the intentional, selfless, sacrificial love that is uniquely of God. We often call agape divine love. It is not just uncommon; it is impossible among fallen humanity.

GOD IS THE SOURCE OF LOVE (4:7)

John plainly states: *"Love is from God."* This indicates love doesn't originate within us. We are not the source; He is. Every authentic expression of love — patience, kindness, forgiveness, sacrifice — comes from God's own being. Just as rivers flow from a spring, true love flows from the heart of God into the lives of His children.

GOD IS THE DEFINITION OF LOVE (4:8)

John makes one of the most powerful statements in all of Scripture: "God is love." If holiness defines His nature and righteousness defines His actions, then love defines His motives.

Love is not just what God does; it's who He is. He shows His goodness through love, and everything He does springs from that goodness — creation, redemption, even judgment.

Imagine trying to measure length without a ruler or weight without a scale. You would have no standard. God's agape love is the true standard, not our culture or your emotions. Without God's agape love, you are at the mercy of the world's distorted view of love.

Why is it so important that John keeps returning to this? God wants you to take a good look at yourself and ask if that active love is clear in your life. This love has only one source. If agape love is present, we are children of God. If it is missing, we are not.

GOD'S ACTIVE LOVE RESTORES (V. 9)

We are nearing the end of hurricane season and haven't had a storm hit us. When disaster strikes, we can take pride in being part of the SBC. We are one of the three or four largest international disaster relief organizations, with over 65,000 volunteers and 1550 disaster units for feeding, showering, laundry, and construction or repair. We do this out of the love of God that motivates us to help.

Where did we learn to help? From our savior

God helps those who hurt.

Does this verse not echo other writings of John? There is similar language and intent to John 3:16

LOVE SENT THE SON

"In this the love of God was made manifest among us, that God sent his only Son into the world." God's love is not an abstract concept. It isn't a warm feeling in heaven or a sentimental idea. It is concrete and visible. Manifested means "it appeared, it was made plain, it became visible in history." God didn't just say "I love you"; He *demonstrated* it by sending Jesus.

"His only Son," points to what is most precious and unique. God sent not an angel, not a prophet, not a representative — but His one and only Son.

And He sent Him "*into the world*," into our brokenness, into our sin, into our mess. The eternal Son left glory to step into our darkness.

I helped serve the elements of the Lord's Supper after the birth of Joshua, and the significance of God sending His son was overwhelming. His sacrifice was more than I could say I would be capable of doing.

LOVE GIVES LIFE

"...so that we might live through him." The purpose of God sending His Son wasn't merely to inspire us, teach us, or reform us. It was to give us life. We were spiritually dead — separated from God, without hope, under judgment. But in Christ we are made alive.

Salvation is not behavior modification — it isn't God cleaning us up a little, teaching us to be nicer, or making us religious.

Salvation is God breathing new life into us by uniting us with His Son.

GOD'S ACTIVE LOVE SATISFIES (V. 10)

What beautiful words John writes, *"Not that we have loved God, but that He loved us."*

GOD TOOK THE INITIATIVE

That small phrase turns everything upside down. Our story doesn't start with us seeking God but with God seeking us. We didn't climb our way to Him; He humbled Himself to us. We didn't love Him first; He loved us first (cf. 1 John 4:19). We must remember **that a**gape is not of this fallen world; it is divine.

This shows the unconditional and initiating nature of God's love. He loved us when we were unlovable — when we were sinners and enemies.

How often do we see videos of criminals attacking police, being shot, and then police working urgently to save their lives? That is God's love — running toward us in our guilt, not away from us.

CHRIST IS THE SATISFACTION FOR SIN

John continues, *"...and sent His Son to be the propitiation for our sins."*

That word "propitiation" means an atoning sacrifice that turns away wrath. The cross satisfied God's holy justice and wrath against sin, so that we could be forgiven and reconciled.

There are two truths we must remember. First, God's love is not sentimental. His love is sacrificial. He didn't simply overlook sin; He fully and finally dealt with it through the death of His Son. Second, God's love is holy. It fulfills justice and extends mercy simultaneously.

Every other kind of love in this world will disappoint or leave us empty — human relationships, pleasures, success, and status. Only God's love in Christ fulfills the deepest needs of our hearts: reconciliation with Him.

GOD'S ACTIVE LOVE PERFECTS (V. 11–12)

I love to grill, but the cleanup is horrible. The sponge soaks up the dirty, oily water. Even when it is dry, if you squeeze it, that nasty comes out. Squeeze a believer and what comes out? God's love

John shares three truths related to God's perfecting love...

IT COMPELS US "Beloved, if God so loved us, we also ought to love one another."

The reasoning is clear and unavoidable. If we have experienced God's infinite, sacrificial love, then how can we withhold love from others? This is not a suggestion; it's an obligation. God's love doesn't end with us. His goal is for it to flow through us.

IT DISPLAYS HIM "No one has ever seen God; if we love one another, God abides in us..." (v. 12a).

We make God's love visible when it is expressed through His people. The world can't see God directly, but they can see Him in the way we treat each other. Think of stained-glass windows when the light shines through, and the beauty is revealed. God's invisible love shines clearly through us.

IT COMPLETES US "...and His love is perfected in us." (v. 12b).

The word "perfected" doesn't mean sinless perfection, but being brought to its intended goal. God's love finds its fulfillment when it reproduces itself in us. His goal is not just to save us, but to shape us into conduits of His love.

The credibility of our salvation is proven not by what we say but by how we love others in action and truth.

13

1 John 4:13-16

W. E. Sangster served as the pastor of *The Queen Street Church* in Scarborough, England. One of the members of his church was a barber and believed it was his duty to witness to his customers. The barber was not always careful. One day, he lathered a man for a shave, picked up the razor, and asked, "Sir, are you prepared to meet your God?" The poor fellow ran away with the lather still on his face.

I believe God loves a faithful witness. I believe one of the greatest honors we can give to the Lord is to be a joyful missionary carrying the gospel message to our lost world. I have never met an immature, disgruntled, hard-hearted believer who was actively sharing their faith.

This is such an important matter that John includes it as one of the tests for our salvation. ***One evidence of authentic salvation is the desire to tell others who Jesus is and what He has done for us.***

Personal evangelism is so profoundly essential a spiritual discipline that John mentions almost in passing—as if he assumes we understand its importance—while discussing the truth of the incarnation.

CONFESSION OF CHRIST
1 John 4:13-16

We are in the midst of an extended passage that serves in many ways as the theological heart of John's letter to the church at Ephesus. He is undermining the message of the false teachers as he proclaims the ***divine identity*** and ***indwelling presence*** of Jesus.

THE TEXT

4:13 John begins *"By this we know..."* pointing to "His love being perfected in us," in verse 12. This acceptance and confession of Jesus' identity at salvation started the process of believers' perfection. We know He is living in us because He is perfecting us.

Our growth in perfection is the work of the Holy Spirit, who dwells in us, and we in Him. John mentions this in verses 13, 15, and 16.

God is not some abstract concept—He really lives and He lives in us.

God is not a distant deity watching to see what will happen in His creation—He involves Himself personally with His people in an intimate manner.

4:14 John is taking the argument against Jesus to the false teachers. They rejected the idea that God would become flesh. John essentially says, "He did, and I was there!" (1:1-4)

One aspect of a Christian's testimony is what occurs in their life. They share their experiences. In a world that dismisses objective truth, your personal experience still matters.

4:15-16 John again discusses the mutual abiding presence of God: Him in us and us in Him. He reminds us that this confirms the truth of the gospel *and*

God's love for us (16a).

There is a chain of thought in these verses that provides a pattern for us to follow.

- John connects the **theological** truth of Jesus' identity to his personal **experience** with Christ. This leads into the committed **practice** of proclaiming the truth.
- Biblical truth is always the essential element in our faith and practice.

This is the preparation Peter calls us to in **1 Peter 3:15**, "But sanctify the Lord God in your hearts, and always be ready to give a defense to everyone who asks you a reason for the hope that is in you, with meekness and fear." (NJKV)

John uses two words that almost get lost in this theological statement regarding the incarnation of Jesus and the assurance of believers. It is the words "testify" and "confesses." These point to the practice of believers sharing their faith through personal testimony with those in their lives.

The notion that believers will be vocal in their faith is baked into the life of a disciple of Jesus.

- Go therefore and make disciples...
- You will be my witnesses...
- Be ready to give a defense...

It takes willful disobedience to Jesus to remain silent about your faith. John tells us it is a test of our salvation. (4:15)

THE BENEFITS OF PERSONAL EVANGELISM

Benefits for the Believer *(Besides obedience and spiritual growth)*

- **Clarity of the Gospel:** Putting God's work into words sharpens understanding of the gospel and personal story.
- **Strengthened Faith:** Sharing your testimony is a reminder of God's work in your life. It reinforces gratitude and confidence in God's ongoing faithfulness (Psalm 107:2).

Benefits for the One Hearing the Gospel *(Besides Salvation)*

- **Hearing the Gospel in Real Life:** A testimony shows how God's truth applies personally, making the gospel tangible and relatable.
- **Breaking Down Barriers:** Your personal story is less confrontational than a debate or argument; it builds trust and opens doors for deeper conversation.

Benefits for the Church *(Besides numerical growth)*

- **Culture of Evangelism:** When members testify, the whole congregation is stirred to greater boldness and faithfulness in witness (Acts 4:31).
- **Evidence of God at Work:** Testimonies serve as living proof that God continues to save, heal, and transform lives.
- **Inspiration for Worship and Prayer:** The church rejoices together at God's victories and is motivated to keep praying for others.

THE EXAMPLE OF FAITHFUL WITNESSES

There are three biblical examples of submissive saints who made a CONFESSION OF CHRIST when the opportunity was presented.

The Shepherds who Announced Jesus' Birth

Luke 2:16-20 *And they went with haste and found Mary and Joseph, and the baby lying in a manger. And when they saw it, they made known the saying that had been told them concerning this child. And all who heard it wondered at what the* *shepherds told them. But Mary treasured up all these things, pondering them in her heart. And* ***the shepherds returned, glorifying and praising God*** *for all they had heard and seen, as it had been told them.*

The shepherds were obedient to go. They were quick to share. They were worshiping when they returned.

- WHY? The shepherds found joy in the privilege to share.
- Who were they in God's kingdom? They were lowly but obedient. They were overlooked by the world but were important to God.

HOW ABOUT YOU? Have you lost the joy of your salvation? Joy speaks.

The Woman at the Well who Found Faith

John 4:28-30 *So the woman left her water jar and went away into town and said to the people, "Come, see a man who told me all that I ever did. Can this be the Christ?" They went out of the town and were coming to him.*

The woman overcame public shame to announce the Messiah. This transformation was so complete that they immediately wanted to investigate. ***A CHANGED LIFE CHANGES LIVES.***

HOW ABOUT YOU? Has your life been so changed by Jesus that those who know you best can see Him the clearest in you?

The Man Who Made Introductions

John 12:20-23 *Now among those who went up to worship at the feast were some Greeks. So these came to Philip, who was from Bethsaida in Galilee, and asked him, "Sir, we wish to see Jesus." Philip went and told Andrew; Andrew and Philip went and told Jesus.*

Philip could have gone directly to Jesus, but he grabbed Andrew first. Andrew loved introducing people to Jesus. He introduced his brother, Peter. (1:35) He introduced the boy with two fish and five loaves to Jesus. (6:5-11)

Because of Andrew: Peter was saved, people were fed, and prophecy was fulfilled.

HOW ABOUT YOU? Is your changed life changing lives?

14

1 John 4:16-21

Nick Saban recounts the story of him and his wife, Terry, returning to the town where they were raised for their high school reunion. As they passed a gas station, he commented that it was the station owned by the family of the young man Terry had dated before Nick.

Smiling, Nick said if she had continued dating the other guy, Terry would now be the wife of a gas station owner.

Terry quickly replied, "If I had married him, he would now be the coach of the Alabama Crimson Tide!"

While it is likely that the other guy would have actually achieved that lofty position in the coaching world, the truth remains: authentic *love impacts the object of its affection.*

When you love someone, your heart, mind, and life are committed to making them better. You want what is best for them and are devoted to achieving it for them.

In our passage, we will see that John explains how God's love impacts the lives of believers.

IMPACT OF GOD'S LOVE
1 John 4:16-21

My goal is that of the Apostles, for listeners to celebrate the love of God by living a life changed by Him.

Let's consider three words that describe how God's love impacts believers...

COMMUNION: God's Love Draws Us In (4:16)

It is almost Christmas. We will quote and sing Isaiah 7:14, "A virgin shall conceive and bear a son, and shall call His name Immanuel."

Immanuel = God with Us. It is now ingrained into our theology and culture. The idea of God in the flesh may be disputed, but it is no longer the horrendous concept it once was in history. The church in Ephesus was in a culture that could not conceive of the idea. Furthermore, their gods did not love them nor seek their friendship.

Greek mythology recounts many tragic tales of the gods' capricious behavior towards humanity. When the hunter Actaeon accidentally stumbled upon Artemis bathing, she capriciously turned him into a stag. His own hunting dogs then tore him apart. His "crime" was being in the wrong place at the wrong time.

Thank God our god is not so capricious and vengeful. John tells us God's very nature is love. It is the motivation for all of His interactions with us. To abide in God's love is to live in Him and Him in us.

John has been teaching twin ideas that are intrinsically connected to God's presence with us. The incarnation teaches us that God became a person. The indwelling teaches us that God became personal.

We see this intimate love of God beautifully portrayed in Psalm 23. David displays so many facets of God's love towards His people. Consider some of the blessings He extends towards us:

- Provisions, *"I shall not want- green pastures and still waters"*
- Peace- *"Paths of righteousness- valley of the shadow of death"*
- Healing- *"Anoint my head with oil"*
- Home- *"I shall dwell in the house of the Lord..."*

Communion means to have something in common. What do we have in common with God? Jesus. Through Jesus, you can have communion, fellowship, and an eternity with God.

CONFIDENCE: God's Love Drives Out Fear (4:17-18)

I chose the word "confidence" since it is the word John uses. Understand, confidence is not arrogance. Arrogance is an *overestimation* of myself. Confidence is a *sober estimation* of myself. Arrogance *overstates* my contribution. Confidence *exalts* the Lord's contribution.

In verses 13-16, John's focus was on God's perfecting love directed *towards* believers. Now, in verses 17-21, his concern is with our love directed *towards* God.

John returns to the familiar word "confidence." This is the third of four uses in the letter. First, in 2:28, he says we have confidence in his 2nd coming. Next, in 3:21-22, he says we have confidence in prayer 3:21-22.

Again, in this third usage of the word, his focus is upon the future. Our confidence in the second coming is evidence of His perfecting love within us. The first verse, 4:17, states the confidence positively. The second verse, 4:18, states the truth negatively.

John's logic is clear. We cannot express both love and terror for the same person. We cannot approach Him in love while fleeing His presence. John says we need not fear because "Fear has to do with punishment." Christ has already been punished in our place.

What does the Bible say about the 2nd Coming of Jesus for those who are not believers? The Scriptures are filled with warnings about the fear of those who choose sin over righteousness. One example is given below:

> **Amos 5:18-20 (NLT)** What sorrow awaits you who say, "If only the day of the Lord were here!" You have no idea what you are wishing for. That day will bring darkness, not light. In that day, you will be like a man who runs from a lion— only to meet a bear. Escaping from the bear, he leans his hand against a wall in his house— and he's bitten by a snake. Yes, the day of the Lord will be dark and hopeless, without a ray of joy or hope.

But this is not so for the redeemed of Christ. This second coming of Jesus is a GLORIOUS event for Christians.

When the trumpet of the Lord shall sound,
And time shall be no more,
And the morning breaks, eternal, bright and fair;
When the saved of earth shall gather
Over on the other shore,
And the roll is called up yonder,
I'll be there.

When the roll is called up yonder,
When the roll is called up yonder
I'll be there.

On that bright and cloudless morning

When the dead in Christ shall rise,
And the glory of His resurrection share;
When His chosen ones shall gather
To their home beyond the skies,
And the roll is called up yonder,
I'll be there.

This is not a song of terror but of joy! We are His children, the objects of His favor. He does not return to *judge* us, but rather, to *rescue* us from this fallen world.

CONNECTION: God's Love Compels Us to Love (4:19-21)

I love theology, though philosophy is not my favorite discipline. Still, the two often intersect. One key overlap is the concept of the Prime Mover—introduced by Aristotle and later developed by Thomas Aquinas.

The problem Aristotle identified is that everything in the world is in motion, yet every motion is caused by something else—a ball rolls because it was kicked, a tree grows because of the sun and the soil. However, this chain of causes cannot extend back indefinitely. Aristotle argued that there must be a beginning, a first cause.

This first cause is unmoved, uncaused, eternal, and perfect. Aristotle identified it with God (he was not a believer)—the One who sets all things in motion and draws them toward their ultimate purpose, not by force but by being the fullness of perfection itself.

In essence, the Prime Mover is the ultimate, uncaused cause—the reason anything exists or moves at all.

In a narrow sense, that is John's message regarding love. *"We love because He first loved us."*

GOD'S LOVE IS PRIOR (V. 19)

John reminds us that "*We love because He first loved us.*" Interestingly, this sentence lacks a direct object (it simply reads, 'We love.'). Should 'God' be added as the direct object, or should it be 'one another'? I believe it's both—you wouldn't love ANYONE if God didn't first surround us with His love.

The foundation of love is never us; it always begins with God. His love existed before we ever thought about Him, before we sought Him, and even before our birth.

In fact, God loved us while we were sinners, rebels, and enemies (Romans 5:8). This shows that our love for God and others isn't something we generate on our own; it's a response to God's initiating love.

GOD'S LOVE IS OUR PROOF (V. 20)

John presses the point even further: *"If anyone says, 'I love God,' and hates his brother, he is a liar."* Those are strong words.

It is possible to say all the right things about loving God while our actions tell a different story. Love for others is the visible proof that our claim to love God is genuine.

Our love for one another is the practical evidence that God's love has taken root in our hearts. Just as fruit proves the healthy life of a tree, love for others proves the reality of our relationship with God. Without this proof, our words about loving God are empty.

GOD'S LOVE IS OUR PRACTICE (V. 21).

The command is plain: love for God requires love for others. God's perfected love moves us from profession to practice. To love God *properly* is to love people *faithfully*.

Just as light proves the presence of the sun, love for others proves the presence of God's love within us.

The ultimate sign that God's love is perfected in us is not what we say about Him, but how we treat those around us. God's love is not just *talk*; it is *transformation.* It overcame sin so we can have fellowship with Him. It satisfied our sin debt, so we need not fear. It compels us to show that love for others.

How about you? Beyond an emotional response to the reality that our sin deserves to be punished, has God's love changed you

15

John 5:1-5

In *The Source*, James Michener tells of Urbaal, a farmer in 2200 B.C. who worshiped two gods—one of death and one of fertility. When priests demand his young son's sacrifice for better crops, Urbaal obeys.

Afterward, they announce that he may spend a week with a temple prostitute. Urbaal's wife watches in horror as her husband's desire overtakes him and he eagerly steps forward. Leaving the temple, she realizes, *"If he had different gods, he would have been a different man."*

It is fiction, but it is correct. Who we worship shapes who we are. Compare the basic tenets of the major religions of the world, and you see the adherents living out their religious faith.

Last week, we saw the impact of God's love in the believer's life. Now we complete the idea by considering the implications of our faith in God upon our lives.

The Impact of Faith

1 John 5:1–5

John has spent most of this letter showing believers what genuine faith *is*. As he reaches the end of his letter, he shows what genuine faith *does.* Faith is not a mere profession — it's a living, active force that changes how we love, how we obey, and how we overcome.

Let's consider three truths about the impact that faith has on our lives...

FAITH PRODUCES LOVE (vv. 1–2)

True faith in Jesus always leads to love. It is impossible to be born of God and not reflect His love. God's nature is love, so being born again into His family means He is reproducing His nature within us—holy, righteous, and loving.

What is the object of our newfound loving affection?

FAITH PRODUCES LOVE FOR GOD

Belief in Jesus as the Christ isn't just intellectual assent — it is a personal trust. We love Him because He first loved us (1 John 4:19).

How do we kindle this affection for God? Dwell on who Jesus is and what He's done for you. For example, think of the sinful woman in Luke 7:36-50 who washed Jesus' feet with her tears. Jesus said, "She loved much because she was forgiven much." Genuine faith sees the greatness of God's mercy and responds in deep love. The cross is the great motivator of our affection.

FAITH PRODUCES LOVE FOR BELIEVERS

John makes a practical point: if you truly love the Father, you will love His children. Faith that unites you to Christ also unites you to His people. To reject your brother or sister is to deny the family of God.

Faith that does not result in love is false faith. Love is not the price of salvation but the proof of it.

FAITH PRODUCES OBEDIENCE (V. 3)

Love and obedience always travel together. You cannot claim to love God and yet disregard His Word.

Consider just a few statements from the Bible:

- **Deuteronomy 10:12–13** "And now, Israel, what does the LORD your God require of you, but to fear the LORD your God, to walk in all his ways, to love him, to serve the LORD your God with all your heart and with all your soul, and to keep the commandments and statutes of the LORD..."
- **John 14:15, 21** "If you love me, you will keep my commandments... Whoever has my commandments and keeps them, he it is who loves me. And he who loves me will be loved by my Father, and I will love him and manifest myself to him."

Why do we recoil at the correlation of love and obedience? We house rebellion in our hearts.

Do not look upon obedience as a surrender of rights or autonomy. Obedience is a declaration of our limited status and abilities. Obedience is a declaration of our trust in the wisdom and goodness of God.

In September of 1954, Paul "Bear" Bryant took nearly 100 Texas A&M football players to Junction, TX, for summer practice. He had been hired in February and found the team to be soft and lacking commitment. The region was in a 4-year drought and reached record highs while the team was working out. Practices began before dawn and lasted until 11 PM with a few water breaks. Players lost 10% of their body weight every day. Every day, players quit. After 10 days of training, fewer than three dozen remained. In 1954, the team went 1-9. Two years later, they won the South West Conference championship. He remade those men.

Gene Stallings played for the Bear, then later coached the Crimson Tide to a national championship, said, "That summer we learned to trust the Bear."

Abraham is called the Father of Faith because his faith led him to obey God when he was asked to leave his homeland and when he was willing to offer Isaac on Mount Moriah. His obedience wasn't perfect, but it was a clear display of faith in action.

Faith doesn't make obedience unnecessary; it makes obedience possible. The Spirit gives us both the desire and the ability to do what pleases God.

FAITH BRINGS VICTORY OVER THE WORLD (VV. 4–5)

Faith not only changes how we love and obey, but it also changes how we *live in a fallen world.*

FAITH BRINGS VICTORY OVER TEMPTATIONS

The "world" in John's writings refers to the system opposed to God — its values, desires, and priorities (1 John 2:15–17). Faith in Jesus gives believers the power to resist these pressures because it changes what we love. When you follow Christ, the world's temptations lose their grip.

Joseph resisted the temptation of Potiphar's wife (Genesis 39) not because he was stronger than others, but because he had faith in the unseen God. He said, "How then could I do this great evil and sin against God?" Faith sees beyond the moment to the presence of God.

FAITH BRINGS VICTORY OVER TRIBULATIONS

Faith not only resists sin — it endures suffering. Jesus said, "In this world you will have tribulation. But take heart; I have overcome the world" (John 16:33). When we trust Him, His victory becomes ours. The apostles in Acts 5 were beaten for preaching Jesus. But, they rejoiced "that they were counted worthy to suffer for His name." Their faith gave them courage that fear could not shake.

Faith doesn't remove the battle, but it guarantees the outcome. In Christ, we are "more than conquerors through Him who loved us" (Romans 8:37).

This victory is the heart of the hymns we often sing:

Encamped along the hills of light,
Ye Christian soldiers rise,
And press the battle ere the night
Shall veil the glowing skies;
Against the foe in vales below
Let all our strength be hurled;
Faith is the victory, we know,
That overcomes the world.

Faith is the victory!
Faith is the victory!
O glorious victory,
That overcomes the world.

Is it worth it? Consider the promise of Jesus, as recorded by John, to believers in Sardis in Revelation 3:1-6. "The one who conquers will be clothed in white garments..."

Faith in Jesus is not static — it is living and active. It *produces love* that unites us with God and with others. It *produces obedience* that transforms our desires and actions. *It brings victory* that overcomes temptation, fear, and the power of the world.

If your faith in Jesus has not changed the way you love, obey, or live, perhaps it is time to ask whether it's real. True faith is more than believing that Jesus exists — it is trusting Him completely, loving Him deeply, and living for Him daily.

16

1 John 5:6-12

I shared the gospel with a man who said he hoped he was saved, but you cannot really know for sure. I tried to show him that God wants us to know, but he never would accept it.

Adrian Rogers said, "There are two classes of people, the saved and the lost, the *SAINTS* and the *AINTS.*" God wants you to know you are a saint.

Believers face a daily barrage of voices challenging everything they know to be true. These attacks aim to undermine our faith in the Lord and make us question our very salvation. This is the fruit of the false teachers, but it is not the will of God. God wants you to KNOW you are secure in your relationship with Him.

In our passage, John tells us God has given a clear testimony that Jesus is His Son. Faith accepts that testimony and finds life in Christ. Unbelief rejects that testimony and remains dead in sin.

John provides six witnesses who affirm the identity of Jesus and the destiny of His people.

BELIEVE THE WITNESS
1 John 5:6-12

John reminds us that faith in Jesus Christ is not blind faith—it rests upon God's own testimony. Christianity is built on evidence—divine, historical, and personal.

We are not without witnesses.

Let's consider the witnesses given to us for belief...

BELIEVE THE WITNESS OF HIS BAPTISM (V. 6–8)

"This is he who came by water and blood—Jesus Christ; not by the water only but by the water and the blood." (v. 6a)

Some believe it refers to baptism and the Lord's Supper, while others see it as His being pierced on the cross when water and blood flowed.

The term "water" refers to Jesus' baptism in the Jordan River. At that moment, God publicly identified Jesus as His Son: "This is my beloved Son, with whom I am well pleased" (Matthew 3:17).

Baptism serves as both an inauguration and an identification. Jesus' baptism marked the start of His earthly ministry. He was led into the wilderness to be tempted and proved to be the superior Adam. His baptism was not a confession of sin but an act of identification with sinners He came to save.

God the Father and the Holy Spirit both bore witness at that moment—the Spirit descending like a dove, the Father speaking audibly from heaven. John's point is that Jesus didn't merely *seem* to be the Son of God; heaven itself confirmed it.

Do you believe that Jesus is the one sent from heaven? His identity was heaven-declared. Faith begins by believing what God has already said about His Son.

BELIEVE THE WITNESS OF HIS CRUCIFIXION (V. 6–8)

Again- *"...not by the water only but by the water and the blood."*

John adds "and the blood" to counter false teachers who claimed that the divine Christ left Jesus before the crucifixion. There, again, God bore witness—darkness covered the land, the temple veil was torn, the earth quaked, and a Roman centurion confessed, "Truly this was the Son of God!" (Matthew 27:54). Jesus' death was not a *tragic accident* but a *divine appointment* to accomplish redemption.

The cross stands as God's loudest declaration of love and truth. To believe in Jesus means trusting in His atoning work — not just His teachings or example. Faith views the cross as God's ultimate evidence of who Jesus is and what He was sent to do.

BELIEVE THE WITNESS OF THE HOLY SPIRIT (V. 6–8)

"And the Spirit is the one who testifies, because the Spirit is the truth."

The Holy Spirit continually witnesses to Jesus' divine identity. He was present at His baptism, involved in His miracles, and strongly affirmed His resurrection.

Jesus said, "When the Helper comes... he will bear witness about me" (John 15:26). The Spirit's testimony is *external* through Scripture and the Church's proclamation. It is also *internal*, convincing the believer's heart.

John emphasizes that "the Spirit is the truth"—His testimony cannot be false or manipulated. When the Spirit convicts your heart of the truth about Jesus, that is God Himself speaking to you. Do not resist His witness—respond in faith.

BELIEVE THE WITNESS OF THE FATHER (V. 9)

"If we receive the testimony of men, the testimony of God is greater, for this is the testimony of God that he has borne concerning his Son."

Human testimony can be persuasive, but God's testimony is perfect and final. God has borne witness through His works, His Word, and His voice from heaven.

- At Jesus' baptism: "This is my beloved Son."
- At the Transfiguration: "Listen to Him."
- At the cross: the supernatural signs confirmed His divine identity.

To reject Jesus is to call God a liar, for it is to reject God's own testimony (v. 10b). If we trust human witnesses in everyday life—news reports, contracts, courtroom verdicts—how much more should we trust the testimony of the eternal God? Faith honors God's word; unbelief insults His character.

BELIEVE THE WITNESS IN YOUR HEART (V. 10)

"Whoever believes in the Son of God has the testimony in himself."

When you believe in Christ, the Holy Spirit places God's witness inside you. *Faith shifts from relying on outside evidence to feeling an internal assurance.* This is the spiritual confirmation—what Paul refers to as "the Spirit himself bears witness with our spirit that we are children of God" (Romans 8:16). The believer doesn't just *agree* with the facts about Jesus; he *experiences* their truth deeply in his heart.

Has the truth of Jesus moved from your mind to your heart? Genuine faith is not just intellectual agreement — it is personal trust. The one who believes *knows* because he has tasted and seen that the Lord is good.

BELIEVE THE WITNESS OF ETERNAL LIFE (VV. 11–12)

"And this is the testimony, that God gave us eternal life, and this life is in his Son. Whoever has the Son has life; whoever does not have the Son of God does not have life."

God's final testimony is that eternal life is found only in His Son. Eternal life is not something we earn or achieve; it is a gift God gave us."

This life is not just an endless existence but a quality of life—spiritual fellowship with God that starts now and lasts forever. To have the Son is to have life. To reject the Son is to stay spiritually dead, no matter how moral or religious one might be.

The dividing line of humanity runs right through this verse. It's not race, wealth, or education—it's Jesus. *Do you have the Son?* That is the most critical question you will ever answer.

John's message is clear: God has not left us in the dark about His Son. He has provided a full and trustworthy testimony—through water, blood, Spirit, the Father's voice, the believer's heart, and the promise of eternal life.

17

1 John 5:13-15

George Washington Carver, born into slavery in Missouri, gained his freedom as a child and was determined to get an education, earning a master's degree in agricultural science from Iowa State. In 1896, he joined the Tuskegee Institute, where he taught and did research for over 40 years.

A humble man of deep Christian faith, Carver believed that science should serve humanity. His research revitalized Southern agriculture by promoting crop rotation and sustainability, showing that wise stewardship of God's creation could lift communities out of poverty.

Carver created over 300 products from peanuts, including peanut flour, coffee substitutes, milk, and soups. He also found industrial uses like dyes, plastics, lubricants, adhesives, and paints. Additionally, he developed household items such as soap, cosmetics, and cleaning products.

Not all of his discoveries were patented or commercially manufactured. His aim was not profit but to improve the lives of everyday farmers.

Carver's diligent efforts brought about unexpected blessings. These were simply side effects of the work he did.

Faith is similar. We hear the gospel—are convicted of our sin and convinced that only Jesus can save us—and we are saved. Along with that joyful blessing come unexpected blessings.

John points to blessings we experience when we hold to the truth of the gospel.

OUR ASSURANCES
1 John 5:13-15

Three simple verses that point to two great blessings that God provides.

What assurances does truth produce in the believer's life?

The Assurance Of The Father's Forgiveness (5:13)

John said, "I write these things to you who believe in the name of the Son of God..."

This message is for believers. His gospel was meant to call the lost to Jesus. His letter aims to confirm the followers of Jesus.

We believe in the security of the believer. We believe that all who come to Christ *stay* in Christ. We do not believe this out of wishful thinking, but based on the biblical text.

Hebrews 10:12,14 But when Christ had offered for all time a single sacrifice for sins, he sat down at the right hand of God.

For by a single offering, he has perfected for all time those who are being sanctified.

Security and assurance are not the same. Security is when God declares I am saved. Assurance is when I believe I am saved. Sin, struggles, and suffering may cause me to question *if I am saved.* God wants me to know.

Two truths related to our forgiveness...

SALVATION IS HIS GIFT

Notice how closely these words echo John 5:24, "Truly, truly, I say to you, whoever hears my word and believes him who sent me has eternal life. He does not come into judgment, but has passed from death to life."

The formulation is clear:

- We believe- We express faith
- In the name- We trust His character
- Son of God- We recognize His divine identity

Salvation is when we trust in the righteous Messiah who is offered as the payment for our sins.

SECURITY IS HIS GUARANTEE

The false teachers in Ephesus have been attacking the very core of salvation. They claim it is not the result of our faith in Jesus' sacrifice but is instead given to a select few through a "secret knowledge" God grants. Turning the tables on them, John uses their word, "know," 39 times in the 104 verses of his letter. He uses it 7 times in these final 9 verses. He now points to one of the most important truths we can know: Are we really saved?

A brief word study: He uses the word "know" as a perfect, active verb. This means the certainty of your salvation is a truth you should hold onto now and always. Once you are redeemed by the blood of Jesus, God never wants you to doubt that you are saved or think you have lost that salvation.

He wants you to *know* Him and the life He has for you. This knowledge produces joy and confidence. Allow me to encourage you with the Word of God on the subject of knowing!

- **John 17:3** And this is eternal life, that they know you, the only true God, and Jesus Christ whom you have sent.
- **Job 19:25-26.** For I know that my Redeemer lives, and at the last he will stand upon the earth. And after my skin has been thus destroyed, yet in my flesh I shall see God
- **Psalm 20:6** Now I know that the Lord saves his anointed; He will answer him from his holy heaven with the saving might of his right hand.
- **2 Timothy 1:12** But I am not ashamed, for I know whom I have believed, and I am convinced that he is able to guard until that day what has been entrusted to me.

This is the knowledge that sustains a believer when his flesh, this world, and the forces of hell rise against him. This is what the assurance of salvation looks like!

THE ASSURANCE OF THE FATHER'S ATTENTION (5:14-15)

Charlie Peacock sang, "My mind played a trick on me..." That trick led him to sin. Don't let your mind deceive you—read the whole verse, not just the fun parts.

Consider again his words, John 5:14: "And this is the confidence that we have toward him, that if we ask anything...he hears us." Why not leave out "according to his will?" We believe it that way.

David writes similar words in Psalm 37:4: "Delight yourself in the Lord, and He will give you the desires of your heart." Like John's words, this can create a distorted image of God if we do not read them correctly. God is not a cosmic Santa Claus waiting to distribute toys. He is our divine shepherd providing for our well-being.

Both of these passages contain qualifiers. David states we receive when we *delight* in God's glory. John states we receive when our prayers are aligned with *God's will.*

Ultimately, this is a passage about prayer. From a human perspective, prayer is an honest conversation with God that produces a continuous awareness of His presence. From the divine perspective, prayer is His constant attention focused on us.

Max Lucado says God focuses his attention upon you as if no one else in the world existed. He says, "If God had a refrigerator, your picture would be on it. If He had a wallet, your photo would be in it. He sends you flowers every spring and a sunrise every morning ... Face it, friend. He's crazy about you!"

These are not random thoughts linked together. God's attentiveness in prayer and His activity in our lives strengthen our confidence in salvation. That's why practicing spiritual disciplines is essential. You never outgrow your dedication to prayer.

In the late 19th century, from the 1850s to the 1890s, crude oil was mainly distilled to produce kerosene. A byproduct of this process was gasoline. It was volatile, flammable, and had few uses. Refiners often discarded or burned gasoline as waste. It was considered useless until the rise of the automobile. Then, both the automotive and oil industries recognized gasoline as a crucial product for powering mobility.

You thought you were just getting a free pass out of hell. The Father was actually welcoming you into His eternal care. He was making you His child, a joint heir with Jesus.

Too often, we view prayer as a way to ask God for "stuff". Prayer is an essential element in shaping us to be like Christ.

Too often, we think of prayer as a clearing house for our wants and needs. When prayer is motivated by a desire to glorify God and is shaped by a desire to follow His will, it takes on a new life. It draws us to enjoy His presence.

Consider your prayer life. Is it only a time to ask for "things" from God?

Reasons to pray BESIDES making requests

1. To worship God for who He is
2. To thank God for what He has done
3. To confess and receive cleansing
4. To align our will with God's will
5. To draw near and enjoy His presence
6. To intercede for others

Are you struggling with your faith? Does the assurance of your salvation seem weak and distant? James 4:8 says, "Draw close to God, and He will draw close to you." If He seems distant, pray.

18

1 John 5:16-21

I had a debate with a friend in college. His position is that we need not pray for the lost since, in his study, the Bible never directs us to do so. His position is that Jesus said to pray for workers to go forth; the field is already prepared.

DISCLAIMER- My friend LOVES Jesus. He loves the lost and often boldly shares the gospel with them. He is a wonderful believer; we just disagreed on this matter.

I always responded to him by reminding him that Paul prayed for the Jews to be saved and even offered his own salvation in exchange for theirs. Today, I can admit my blindness on the matter. I never thought about this passage. John tells us we are to pray for the lost.

PRAYING FOR THE FALLEN
1 John 5:16-21

We use directional language to communicate spiritual truth:

- The Father is ABOVE His creation
- The Jews went UP to Jerusalem
- Joseph was brought DOWN to Egypt

- Adam and Eve FELL into sin
- The Lord raised the Psalmist UP from the pit when He saved him.

We still have friends and family in sin. They have fallen. We must pray and proclaim to see them saved. This passage is challenging. Simple and clear directives and encouragements surround a difficult statement.

Let's consider the main theme of the passage. At its core, the issue is sin. The first enemy we must confront is always sin. It is persistent, pervasive, and present in every person.

A DEFINITION: Sin is a spiritual deficiency present in everyone that prevents us from being righteous in both actions and character. It is a separation from God, humanity, and ourselves. It is rebellion that manifests as disobedience to God's law, rejection of His authority, and aversion to His holy nature.

The Bible teaches that sin entered the world when Adam and Eve chose to violate God's command not to eat from the tree of the knowledge of good and evil. Their nature was corrupted, and this corruption is passed down to their descendants. All of humanity is born with a sinful nature that influences our thoughts and actions. Therefore, we are not sinners because we do wrong; we do wrong because we are sinners.

Sin is deeply rooted in humanity. It plays a part in shaping our character. According to Charles Ryrie, the sin nature is "that capacity which all men have to serve and please self. Sin is the capacity to leave God out of one's life."

Using the biblical text as guidance, we know that sin is missing the mark, corruption or pollution, rebellion and trespass, spiritual and moral bondage. The result is always the same. Sin produces death—every time and in every person.

- **Romans 5:12** Therefore, just as sin came into the world through one man, and death through sin, and so death spread to all men because all sinned.
- **Romans 6:23** For the wages of sin is death, but the free gift of God is eternal life in Christ Jesus our Lord.

Let's examine the passage. John continues his explanation of how we can have confidence in prayer by providing an illustration. The main focus is on the confidence we have, not the illustration he presents.

This passage is hard to interpret. We understand more about what it doesn't mean than what it does. It would have been helpful if he had elaborated, but he did not.

Notice the structure. Like a funnel that widens as he speaks, the passage starts with a specific example and gradually moves toward a universal truth.

- 5:16 A Specific Truth
- 5:17 A General Truth
- 5:18 A Doctrinal Truth
- 5:19 A Universal Truth

You can reverse the funnel and start broad and work towards the specific truth John is using as an illustration.

The **DOCTRINAL TRUTH of verse 18** has already been addressed. John does not say believers never commit any sin; he says we do not continue in habitual sin.

1 John 3:6-9. No one who abides in him keeps on sinning; no one who keeps on sinning has either seen him or known him. Little children, let no one deceive you. Whoever practices righteousness is righteous, as he is righteous. Whoever makes a practice of sinning is of the devil, for the devil has been sinning from the beginning. The reason the Son of God appeared was to destroy the works of the devil. No one born of God makes a practice of sinning, for God's seed abides in him; and he cannot keep on sinning, because he has been born of God.

The **UNIVERSAL TRUTH of verse 19** has been spoken by the apostles. As the Greeks came seeking Jesus during the passion week, he proclaimed the coming victory He would win through the cross. He makes a statement regarding the rule of the sinful world

John 12:30. Now is the judgment of this world; now will the ruler of this world be cast out.

Again, Paul speaks of the rule of this fallen world: 2 Corinthians 4:4. In their case the god of this world has blinded the minds of the unbelievers, to keep them from seeing the light of the gospel of the glory of Christ, who is the image of God.

May I say, these are not difficult truths for us. We often see them in the Scriptures. Our challenge is 5:16-17. What does John mean?

There are several possible interpretations. I will offer three options that I do not necessarily endorse but which demonstrate the range of ideas. First is the Roman Catholic view of VENAL SINS—those that can be pardoned—and MORTAL SINS—those that lead to spiritual death. A major challenge is that Scripture teaches all sin is mortal and results in hell.

A second possibility is that John refers to the consequences of a specific, literal sin, such as Ananias and Sapphira committed in Acts 5. This may also include the immoral man in 1st Corinthians whose flesh was to be destroyed so the spirit could be saved. This would be a sin the church in Ephesus was aware of but has not recorded for us.

Finally, some believe this concerns blasphemy against the Holy Spirit, as Jesus mentions in Matthew 12. This is certainly possible, but John does not mention the Holy Spirit in this passage.

I appreciate how Dr. David Jackman addresses the difficulty we face with this text.

> *Many sensitive Christians have suffered great anguish, and still do, imagining some particular sin of theirs to be unforgivable, or that in a rash moment they might commit the unpardonable sin. Indeed, because this sin has been surrounded by so much 'mystery', it has been the object of so much fear. That cannot be helpful, either to our understanding or to our spiritual health. Perhaps the most mysterious element is that such a sin can exist at all, given that we have such a gracious God who loves to pardon and to reconcile. A Christian minister may rightly try to counsel a distressed Christian by pointing out that any real dread is a sure indication that he is not guilty of this sin.* **One certainty must be that those who are most guilty are least concerned about their state.**

So, how do we understand John's words? His main point is that only those who believe Jesus is the Son of God have eternal life (5:5,13). Therefore, the sin that leads to death—the one that separates the sinner from God's life—must be the denial of this saving truth.

It echoes the warnings of Hebrews.

Hebrews 2:1-3. Therefore, we must pay much closer attention to what we have heard, ***lest we drift away from it***. For since the message declared by angels proved to be reliable, and every transgression or disobedience received a just retribution, ***how shall we escape if we neglect such a great salvation?***

Hebrews 6:4-6. For it is impossible, in the case of those who have once been enlightened, who have tasted the heavenly gift, and have shared in the Holy Spirit, and have tasted the goodness of the word of God and the powers of the age to come, and then have fallen away, to restore them again to repentance, since they are crucifying once again the Son of God to their own harm and holding him up to contempt.

Hebrews paints a painful picture of people who knew better. They heard the truth. They were convinced and convicted by the truth. They walked away because of the demands of the truth. They have NO HOPE.

This is the heart of Jesus' Parable of the Four Soils. Two soils showed a brief sign of life, but it was not salvation. John says those who have rejected Jesus for another messiah have no hope.

This illustrates a greater truth he began speaking of in 5:14-15. "If we ask Him anything according to His will, He will hear us." And "We know that we have the requests that we have asked of Him." We must be interceding for fellow believers, confident that the Lord hears and cares. It is a call for prayer warriors.

He concludes with two verses (20-21) that summarize the book. We know who Jesus is. We know we are in Him. We know we can keep righteous and avoid idols. We worship HIM!

Finally, let us consider how to pray for the lost. I offer a well-known acrostic to guide our prayers.

PRAY FOR THEIR H.E.A.R.T.

Pray for receptive HEARTS (Luke 8:5,12)

Pray for their spiritual EYES to be open (Matthew 13:15)

Pray for God's ATTITUDE toward sin (John 16:8)

Pray the person to be RELEASED to believe (2 Corinthians 10:3-4)

Pray for a TRANSFORMING life (Romans 12:1-2)

Who do you know who is lost and in need of prayer?

19

1 John 5:13 "Five Tests of Salvation"

One of my former pastors, Don Long, would often ask the question, "Do you know that you know that you know that when you die, you are going to heaven?" Are you certain of your salvation?

He did not want the saved to fear they were lost, but he also did not want the lost to mistakenly believe they were saved. There is nothing worse than believing you are headed for heaven when you are actually headed for hell.

John's position, as he repeatedly mentions in this letter, is that every believer should have absolute certainty that they are saved. More than wishful thinking, there are five absolute evidences of authentic salvation.

FIVE TESTS OF SALVATION
1 John 5:13

John makes this declarative statement that should be memorized and celebrated by every follower of Jesus Christ. His words assure Christians that salvation is real. It can be proven, and it is eternal.

But, unfortunately, many have experienced a religious event and never entered into a saving relationship with the Son of God.

First, let's consider some of the sources of this false faith...

FALSE SECURITY

Everything on this list is good. They are certainly expected to be present in salvation. However, these items alone, or even when grouped together, are not enough to validate authentic faith.

Being able to identify the date when you made a decision for Christ. This may include recalling the events surrounding the response, such as feelings of conviction over sin, the emotional response, baptism, and uniting with the church.

Being able to demonstrate attendance, participation in activities, and acts of service on behalf of the Church

> *Are there more chilling words than those of Jesus in Matthew 7:21-23? "Not everyone who says to me, 'Lord, Lord,' will enter the kingdom of heaven, but the one who does the will of my Father who is in heaven. On that day many will say to me, 'Lord, Lord, did we not prophesy in your name, and cast out demons in your name, and do many mighty works in your name?' And then will I declare to them, 'I never knew you; depart from me, you workers of lawlessness.'*

Being drawn to spiritual matters. It may be a sense of conviction when a message is preached or an interest in spiritual disciplines, such as prayer and Bible study. It can also lead to extensive knowledge.

Again, none of these are wrong and should be evident in every believer, but they are not sufficient evidence of one who has been redeemed.

John addressed a congregation that was being misled by false teachers. These godless men were proclaiming a perverted gospel. It caused believers to question their standing with Jesus. John writes to instruct believers HOW they can know they are saved.

Let's consider the biblical tests of authentic salvation...

THE TEST OF PERSONAL HOLINESS

1st John 1:6-7 If we say we have fellowship with him while we walk in darkness, we lie and do not practice the truth. But if we walk in the light, as he is in the light, we have fellowship with one another, and the blood of Jesus his Son cleanses us from all sin.

1 John 2:15-17, 29 Do not love the world or the things in the world. If anyone loves the world, the love of the Father is not in him. For all that is in the world—the desires of the flesh and the desires of the eyes and pride of life—is not from the Father but is from the world. And the world is passing away along with its desires, but whoever does the will of God abides forever.

1 John 2:29 If you know that he is righteous, you may be sure that everyone who practices righteousness has been born of him.

Two truths these words remind us: God's chief attribute is holiness, and He expects his children to pursue this holiness in their own lives. Leviticus 21:8 and 1 Peter 1:16 tell us, "Be holy as I am holy." And my struggle with holiness is often influenced by the world. I emulate what I see in the media.

HOLINESS IS TO BE PERSONAL. My motives, desires, and affections are to be pure. My desire is to keep a clean heart that honors God.

HOLINESS IS TO BE PRACTICAL. As a believer, I have to be convinced of what I allow to influence my heart and mind. This includes entertainment. It includes the people who influence my life. Solomon's son, Rehoboam, got into trouble because his counselors were not godly

Do you live out a HOLY life? Take the pulpit test. Would you be able to act out your life on the platform in front of the congregation?

THE TEST OF OBEDIENCE

1 John 2:3-6 And by this we know that we have come to know him, if we keep his commandments. Whoever says "I know him" but does not keep his commandments is a liar, and the truth is not in him, but whoever keeps his word, in him truly the love of God is perfected. By this we may know that we are in him: whoever says he abides in him ought to walk in the same way in which he walked.

1 John 3:24 Whoever keeps his commandments abides in God, and God in him. And by this we know that he abides in us, by the Spirit whom he has given us.

There is a reason why REBELLION and TRESPASS are words used to describe sin in Scripture. The natural disposition of my heart is disobedience

Obedience has positive and negative aspects and presents a twofold blessing

The NEGATIVE ASPECT of Obedience. It diverts us away from activities that are harmful. One example is how the Scriptures warn against the dangers of alcohol

> ***Proverbs 23:29-35*** *Who has woe? Who has sorrow? Who has strife? Who has complaining? Who has wounds without cause? Who has redness of eyes? Those who tarry long over wine; those who go to try mixed wine. Do not look at wine when it is red, when it sparkles in the cup, and goes down smoothly. In the end, it bites like a serpent and stings like an adder. Your eyes will see strange things, and your heart utter perverse things. You will be like one who lies down in the midst of the sea, like one who lies on the top of a mast. "They struck me," you will say, "but I was not hurt; they beat me, but I did not feel it. When shall I awake? I*

must have another drink."

The POSITIVE ASPECT of Obedience. It shapes our hearts and minds to reflect Christ. As I obey the instructions to love, pray, minister, and witness, I take on the ministry of the Savior.

I will not ask if you struggle with obedience—you do. You are in the flesh, which is at war with His Spirit in us. The question is whether you go beyond the struggle to obedience.

Obedience is evidence of love for Jesus and the presence of His Holy Spirit.

THE TEST OF LOVE

1st John 2:9-11 Whoever says he is in the light and hates his brother is still in darkness. Whoever loves his brother abides in the light, and in him there is no cause for stumbling. But whoever hates his brother is in the darkness and walks in the darkness, and does not know where he is going, because the darkness has blinded his eyes.

John also mentions this in 3:14; 4:7; and 4:20-21

This may be the hardest to recognize since love is not always obvious. Love for the brethren is not simply attending the same church. It is not simply tolerance or friendliness.

LOVE IS STRIVING FOR ANOTHER'S EDIFICATION. How can I help you build up, become better?

LOVE REVEALS ITSELF. It is seen in how we minister and forgive others,

LOVE IS FOSTERED. In sacrificing oneself for others.

THE TEST OF SINLESSNESS

1 John 3:6-8 (ESV) No one who abides in him **keeps on sinning**; no one who **keeps on sinning** has either seen him or known him. Little children, let no one deceive you. Whoever practices righteousness is righteous, as he is righteous. Whoever **makes a practice of sinning** is of the devil, for the devil has been sinning from the beginning.

> *What a strange kind of salvation they do desire that care not for holiness. They would have their sins forgiven, not that they may walk with God in love in time to come, but that they may practice their enmity against him without any fear of punishment.* ***–Walter Marshall 1692***

John does NOT mince his words. Do not call yourself a Christian if you practice habitual sin. The Holy Spirit convicts the believer when he sins. The believer understands that sin is not simply **wrong** but it is **bad** (corrupt and evil)

Four ways to prevent sin from becoming a habit:

1. **Confess and Repent Quickly.** Don't delay repentance. The longer sin remains unconfessed, the deeper its roots grow.
2. **Identify and Cut Off the Source of Temptation.** Habitual sin flourishes where triggers are easy to access or frequent. Jesus' words on gouging out the eye (Matthew 5:29) remind us that drastic measures are sometimes needed. Remove triggers—delete apps, avoid certain places, change routines, or limit contact with tempting influences.
3. **Replace Sinful Patterns with Righteous Ones.** You can't just "stop" sinning—you must fill that space with something holy. Replace angry words with prayer, lust with gratitude, and greed with generosity. When the heart is occupied with righteousness, sin loses its foothold.
4. **Stay in Genuine Fellowship.** Isolation fuels sin; community weakens it. God designed the church to help us bear one another's burdens and pursue holiness together.

THE TEST OF TESTIMONY

1st John 4:15 Whoever confesses that Jesus is the Son of God, God abides in him, and he in God.

There are no silent saints. The believer has an intentional witness to tell the world. We tell them Jesus is the only way to have our sins forgiven. Jesus is the savior who has transformed our lives.

My goal is NOT to cause anyone to doubt what God has done in their lives. Struggling with temptation is NOT evidence of being lost. It may be lacking the power to resist and avoid sin. It is definitely lacking a DESIRE to resist sin. Being weak in a particular area does not mean you are lost. However, lacking an affection for God, His glory, His kingdom, and the church is.

20

2nd John

My aunt married into a family of Primitive Baptists. My grandmother, who was not always the most articulate when communicating with others, wasn't sure how to address the pastor officiating the service.

Following the wedding rehearsal, my grandmother wanted to ask him a question about the service. Not sure how to address him, she asked, rather bluntly, "Do you call yourself a preacher?"

He smiled and replied, "I do, but I can't say my congregation does."

What defines a preacher? What about a Christian church or a disciple of Jesus Christ? What distinguishes Christianity from the Jehovah's Witnesses, Mormons, Jews, and Muslims?

It is the TRUTH. It is the validity of the message proclaimed and believed from scripture. We will see that John said that the truth of the gospel defines a congregation of believers.

DEFINED BY THE TRUTH

2 John

My desire is that of the apostle's, for believers to commit to living the truth of the gospel as proof of their salvation. How do we do that?

Let's consider the WAYS a believer lives defined by the TRUTH

A Believer Loves the Truth (vv. 1–3)

I can list four recent news stories where the information was not incorrect; it was incomplete. Key facts were omitted to make the person making the claim appear righteous rather than accurate. It proves the saying I heard years ago: 'If you ignore the news, you are uninformed. If you listen to the news, you are misinformed.'

John's introduction is brief but loaded with encouragement and direction for believers in a truth-challenged culture.

NOTICE THE TONE: John is "the elder." It is one of three titles associated with his leadership of the church. He is a pastor who tends to the needs of the congregation. He is the bishop or overseer who manages the church's affairs. He is the ELDER who leads with wisdom and maturity.

The "elect lady' and her children seem to be a respectful title for the congregation and its members. This is a letter from a caring pastor to the church he loves.

NOTICE THE LANGUAGE: He uses the word "truth" four times in three verses. We must ask, what exactly is "truth?" Chuck Colson defines truth as "That which accords with reality." Truth is the message of the gospel and the summation of Christian doctrine. Truth is Jesus. It is embodied in our savior, who is the way, the truth, and the life.

In this context, John speaks of the truth of Jesus' identity and ministry. It is the familiar target of false teachers.

NOTICE THE CONNECTION: John mentions "love" twice. It is linked in both instances to truth. He is telling us that when we learn the gospel, we come to understand the truth about who Jesus is and are transformed into ambassadors of His love.

NOTICE THE BLESSINGS: As is common in 1st century letters, the author pronounces a blessing upon the recipients. This threefold blessing is uniquely Christian.

- **Grace** to the guilty and undeserving
- **Mercy** to the needy and helpless
- **Peace** to those out of harmony with God, man, and themselves

Truth and love are the qualities that validate these three virtues. Truth and love are not distinct matters. They are interdependent aspects of God's nature.

A Believer Lives the Truth (vv. 4–6)

John now begins the meat of the message he has for the congregation. He again mentions truth once and love three times. But, he adds another word for our consideration: "**command.**" John uses the word four times in three verses. We are commanded to walk in truth and love.

Why do we recoil at the idea of a command or call to obedience? We live in sinful flesh that is prone to rebellion. Every command of God flows from His love and leads to our good. We are the products of a culture that resists authority. True freedom is found in surrender, not self-rule (John 8:31–32; Romans 6:17–18). We have a shallow view of grace. Grace doesn't free us ***from*** obedience — it frees us ***for*** obedience.

We say the Bible is our guide for faith and practice.

Gathering together 1-6, we see the correlation of truth and love. Truth and love are not distinct matters. They are interdependent aspects of God's nature.

- **Truth gives love integrity.** Without truth, love loses its moral center. The world defines love as tolerance or affirmation, but Christian love is rooted in reality—what is right and true in God's eyes.
- **Love gives truth tenderness.** Truth without love becomes harsh and condemning. Love without truth becomes weak and compromising.
- **Together, truth and love reflect Jesus.** He was "full of grace and truth" (John 1:14). In Him, we see the perfect harmony of conviction and compassion, holiness and mercy.

A Believer Looks for the Truth (vv. 7–11)

Over the past few years, I have become familiar with the term "platforming." In its current usage, the term refers to the act of giving someone visibility, influence, or legitimacy by providing them access to an audience or public forum.

Recently, a conservative talk show host welcomed an avowed Nazi who calls Hitler a hero and denies the holocaust to be interviewed on his show. The host had only a passing interest in challenging the Nazi.

Believers must be cautious about who they support. Love doesn't mean we give everyone the benefit of the doubt or believe the best in them when their message and behavior oppose the gospel.

In Matthew 10, Jesus sends the 12 to proclaim that the kingdom of heaven is at hand. They were to minister and meet the needs of the people. He advises them on their lodging:

And whatever town or village you enter, find out who is worthy in it and stay there until you depart. As you enter the house, greet it. And if the house is worthy, let your peace come upon it, but if it is not worthy, let your peace return to you. And if anyone will not receive you **or listen to your words**, shake off the dust from your feet when you leave that house or town. Truly, I say to you, it will be more bearable on the day of judgment for the land of Sodom and Gomorrah than for that town. *(Matt 10:11–15)*

Jesus is not some soft-spoken game show host giving us another spin of the wheel. He is truth, and truth divides.

- **The Jehovah's Witnesses** preach a corrupt gospel based upon works and good deeds. They preach a degraded Jesus, one who is not eternal nor God incarnate.
- **The Mormons** preach a corrupt gospel based upon works and good deeds. They preach a degraded Jesus, one who is not eternal nor God incarnate. It is a different degradation, but it is still counter to the Bible.

I have one modicum of respect for the Jehovah's Witnesses; they know they are not Christian. The Mormons want more than anything to be viewed as authentic Christianity. They are not.

John issues a strong command: Do not receive or greet those who bring this false doctrine that degrades Jesus (vv. 10-11). Understand this command within its cultural context: Greeting and receiving someone in your home signified *endorsing their teaching.*

Christians are called to be both loving and discerning; their love must be informed by truth. Anyone who welcomes a deceiver shares in their sin (v. 11).

A Believer Longs for the Truth (vv. 12–13)

Tom Kinchens, then president of The Baptist College of Florida, told our freshmen class that 50% would drop out of college before graduation. The single most common factor is a lack of personal connections with fellow students and teaching staff. Ministry—and the Christian faith—is not for

Lone Rangers.

John ends with a personal note. The entire letter has balanced two great themes: *truth and love.* Both are essential to a healthy Christian life and a faithful church. He uses relational language to remind us that *truth and love are never just private virtues*—they are meant to be lived out within community.

For John, doctrine and fellowship go hand in hand. A Christian who loves the truth cannot be indifferent to the health of the church. When we walk in truth, we contribute to the joy, unity, and holiness of the church family.

Fellowship makes our "Joy Complete" (v. 12). Joy thrives in fellowship. He could have written more. He had "much to write," yet he preferred personal presence to written words. Why? Because truth and love are most fully experienced *in a relationship.*

In the ancient world, letters were a necessary but impersonal means of communication. We live in a digital age of emails, texts, livestreams, and social media. While useful, they can't replace *face-to-face* fellowship. Gathering—singing, praying, hearing the Word—completes joy.

That's what authentic Christian fellowship looks like. It's not built on shared interests, personalities, or traditions—it's built on the truth of the gospel and the love that flows from it.

How do we cultivate a longing for the truth?

- **Value truth-centered relationships.** Build friendships centered on Scripture, prayer, and a shared devotion to Christ, rather than just social connections.
- **Prioritize presence.** Be present with the people of God. Attend worship. Join the fellowship. Share life face-to-face. That's where joy grows.
- **Celebrate the wider family of faith.** Remember that our local church is

part of a global body, united by the same truth and the same Savior.

21

3rd John

The Normandy Park Baptist Church GO! Mission offering is simple. It is 1% more. God's word calls for us to give 10% as a tithe. The GO! fund asks to increase that to 11%, with the additional 1% going to missions support. It has doubled our Annie Armstrong and Lottie Moon annual offerings. Your simple 1% increase in giving also allows us to support faith missionaries such as Zack Wing.

Sometimes we make the Christian faith more complicated than it is. God uses simple things to help us grow and to glorify himself: simple obedience, simple faith, and simple offerings. Often, these offerings are not about money. One offering that can truly impact the kingdom is hospitality. Just opening our homes, hearts, and lives to fellow believers can truly change someone's life.

2nd John is a letter to a church warning against welcoming deceivers.

3rd John is a letter to an individual, warning against rejecting missionaries.

In this short, straightforward letter, John explained how simple hospitality helps support Kingdom missions.

Support for Missions
3rd John

John explains how a Christian supports missions. His goal, and ours, is for believers to commit themselves to supporting missions in simple ways they can. Let's explore ways a believer actively supports Christian missions.

To support missions, a believer will:

BE A MISSIONARY (1-4)

Every Christian is called to be a missionary for the gospel of Jesus Christ.

There was a time when we carried letters of introduction. They were used to introduce a friend or acquaintance to someone else. The idea was that our good opinion of a person was being communicated to someone who was a stranger to them.

What a wonderful introduction to Gaius. John loves him in truth (v.1), and he was walking in truth (v.4). Reflecting 2nd John, the greatest praise the Apostle can give this man is that his life and relationships were centered on the gospel.

Gaius was living out Malachi 2:6, in which the prophet used Levi as an example of godliness for the priests to follow.

Malachi 2:6 "True instruction was in his mouth, and no wrong was found on his lips. He walked with me in peace and uprightness, and he turned many from iniquity."

Malachi identified four traits that describe a godly man:

- He is a student of scripture
- He lives with integrity

- He sought the presence of the Lord in his life
- He led people to salvation

Gaius LOVED missionaries because he LIVED on mission.

From the mid-70s to the late 90s, the SBC had a missions emphasis called the **Bold Mission Thrust**. It was a renewed emphasis on evangelism, church planting, and international missions. It worked! There was an increase in baptisms worldwide.

By the early 2000s, a new movement emerged. The label for this movement was "missional living," which steps back from a typical missions discussion. The idea is that we are ALL MISSIONARIES. We should see our workplaces, communities, and families as the mission field prepared for us by God. We should approach them in the same way a missionary does on foreign soil.

The mission does not begin when your foot lands on foreign soil. The mission does not begin when you connect with people from different cultures.

The mission begins when your foot hits the floor in the morning. The mission begins when you connect with anyone everywhere.

Remember: God uses simple things to grow us and glorify himself —simple obedience, simple faith, simple offerings—changing the world.

ENCOURAGE MISSIONARIES (5-8)

Grace Silas was a widow at Cedar Creek during my childhood. Her daughter, Marie, and son-in-law, Frank, served as missionaries in Central America, working as nurses and church planters. We make care packages for their family almost every year. They could buy the essentials on the mission field, but there were extras—treats—that they couldn't get there. I remember loading up packages of Oreos and pudding cups for their children.

Encouragement can be found in small actions and contributions. Gaius simply opened his home to missionaries in the area. He, apparently, did this regularly.

Mark chapter two narrates how four men brought their crippled friend to Jesus. They carried him on a cot to Peter's house, which was already crowded. They climbed onto the roof, made a hole, and lowered him down.

- It was a modest gesture—carry the friend to Jesus
- It was a costly gesture—roofs aren't cheap
- It was a remarkable gesture—When Jesus saw THEIR faith, he healed the crippled man.

Gaius followed their example

- He offered a modest blessing—he opened his home
- He offered a costly blessing—he provided meals
- He offered a remarkable blessing—the missionaries testified of his blessings

God uses simple offerings to change lives.

CHECK YOUR HEART (9-11)

No one wants to be forgotten. I ran into a college professor ten years after graduating from The Baptist College of Florida, and he immediately recognized me, smiled, and called me by name.

I fear that sometimes it's better to be forgotten. Diotrephes would likely wish his name were *not* recorded in Scripture. He would prefer not to be remembered as a bad believer.

NOTE: He is a believer. He is a church member. He is in sin.

John levels four charges against him:

- He is conceited and wants to be first. Diotrephes seeks authority and recognition for himself rather than submitting to godly oversight.
- He talks wicked nonsense. He gossips or defames John and the missionaries, undermining their credibility
- He is inhospitable. Diotrephes blocks traveling missionaries from receiving help, lodging, or support—contradicting the biblical call to hospitality (Rom. 12:13; Heb. 13:2).
- He opposes others extending hospitality. He expels or rejects those who support John or the missionaries, exercising authoritarian control over the church.

Again, I say, He is a believer. He is a church member. He is in sin.

Why oppose the missionaries? So no one can oppose him. Ungodly behavior *fears* godliness and grace.

STAY CONNECTED (12-15)

There is a thought that Gaius may have been swayed by Diotrephes. So, to address the problem, John turns his attention to Demetrius. John said, "I hope to come to you and talk face to face..." because fellowship makes our "Joy Complete." Truth and love are most fully experienced *in a relationship.*

That's what authentic Christian fellowship looks like. It's not built on shared interests, personalities, or traditions—it's built on the truth and ministry.

As we support missionaries, we grow in our love for them.

As we support missionaries, we grow in love for each other!

We diminish the value of our gifts. The Lord does not. The gospel of Luke records how Jesus blessed a woman who gave a simple gift.

Luke 21:1-4 Jesus looked up and saw the rich putting their gifts into the
offering box, **2** and he saw a poor widow put in two small copper coins. **3**
And he said, "Truly, I tell you, this poor widow has put in more than all of
them. **4** For they all contributed out of their abundance, but she out of her
poverty put in all she had to live on."

You change lives through faithful generosity with the simple offerings you make with your life.

www.ingramcontent.com/pod-product-compliance
Lightning Source LLC
LaVergne TN
LVHW010624100826
845148LV00014B/3096
* 9 7 8 1 7 3 6 1 4 5 4 6 3 *